SERIES

(ex•ploring)

1. Investigating in a systematic way: examining. 2. Searching into or ranging over for the purpose of discovery.

SERIES

(ex•ploring)

1. Investigating in a systematic way: examining. 2. Searching into or ranging over for the purpose of discovery.

Getting Started with
Windows 7

Robert T. Grauer

Lynn Hogan | Mary Anne Poatsy

Prentice Hall
Upper Saddle River   London   Singapore
Toronto   Tokyo   Sydney   Hong Kong   Mexico City

Editor in Chief: Michael Payne
Acquisitions Editor: Samantha McAfee
Product Development Manager: Eileen Bien Calabro
Editorial Project Manager: Meghan Bisi
Development Editor: Laura Town
Editorial Assistant: Marilyn Matos
AVP/Director of Online Programs, Media: Richard Keaveny
AVP/Director of Product Development: Lisa Strite
Editor-Digital Learning & Assessment: Paul Gentile
Product Development Manager-Media: Cathi Profitko
Editorial Media Project Manager: Alana Coles
Production Media Project Manager: John Cassar
Director of Marketing: Kate Valentine
Marketing Manager: Tori Olson Alves
Marketing Coordinator: Susan Osterlitz
Marketing Assistant: Darshika Vyas
Senior Managing Editor: Cynthia Zonneveld
Associate Managing Editor: Camille Trentacoste
Production Project Manager: Ruth Ferrera-Kargov
Manager of Rights & Permissions: Shannon Barbe
Senior Operations Specialist: Diane Peirano
Senior Art Director: Jonathan Boylan
Cover Design: Jonathan Boylan
Cover Illustration/Photo: Courtesy of Shutterstock® Images
Composition: GGS Higher Education Resources, a Division of PreMedia Global, Inc.
Full-Service Project Management: GGS Higher Education Resources, a Division of PreMedia Global, Inc.
Typeface: 10.5/12.5 Minion

Credits and acknowledgments borrowed from other sources and reproduced, with permission, in this textbook appear on appropriate page within text.

Microsoft® and Windows® are registered trademarks of the Microsoft Corporation in the U.S.A. and other countries. Screen shots and icons reprinted with permission from the Microsoft Corporation. This book is not sponsored or endorsed by or affiliated with the Microsoft Corporation.

Pearson Prentice Hall™ is a trademark of Pearson Education, Inc.
Pearson® is a registered trademark of Pearson plc
Prentice Hall® is a registered trademark of Pearson Education, Inc.

Pearson Education Ltd., London
Pearson Education Singapore, Pte. Ltd.
Pearson Education, Canada, Ltd.
Pearson Education–Japan
Pearson Education Australia PTY, Limited

Pearson Education North Asia Ltd., Hong Kong
Pearson Educación de Mexico, S.A. de C.V.
Pearson Education Malaysia, Pte. Ltd.
Pearson Education, Upper Saddle River, New Jersey

Many of the designations by manufacturers and seller to distinguish their products are claimed as trademarks. Where those designations appear in this book, and the publisher was aware of a trademark claim, the designations have been printed in initial caps or all caps.

10 9 8 7 6 5 4 3 2 1

Prentice Hall
is an imprint of

www.pearsonhighered.com

ISBN-13: 978-0-13-508826-5
ISBN-10: 0-13-508826-7

DEDICATIONS

I wholeheartedly dedicate this book to my father in recognition of
his support, guidance, and encouragement. His steady influence
and unwavering confidence continue to be an inspiration in
my life. He is truly my hero.

Lynn Hogan

For my husband Ted, who unselfishly continues to take on more
than his fair share to support me throughout this process; and for
my children, Laura, Carolyn, and Teddy, whose encouragement and
love have been inspiring.

Mary Anne Poatsy

ABOUT THE AUTHORS

Lynn Hogan

Lynn Hogan has taught in the Computer Information Systems area at Calhoun Community College for 29 years. She is the author of *Practical Computing* and has contributed chapters for several computer applications textbooks. Primarily teaching in the areas of computer literacy and computer applications, she was named Calhoun's outstanding instructor in 2006. She received an M.B.A. from the University of North Alabama and a Ph.D. from the University of Alabama. Lynn resides in Alabama with her husband and two daughters.

Mary Anne Poatsy, MBA, CFP

Mary Anne is a senior faculty member at Montgomery County Community College, teaching various computer application and concepts courses in face-to-face and online environments. She holds a B.A. in psychology and education from Mount Holyoke College and an M.B.A. in finance from Northwestern University's Kellogg Graduate School of Management.

Mary Anne has more than 11 years of educational experience, ranging from elementary and secondary education to Montgomery County Community College, Muhlenberg College, and Bucks County Community College, as well as training in the professional environment. Before teaching, she was vice president at Shearson Lehman Hutton in the Municipal Bond Investment Banking Department.

Dr. Robert T. Grauer

Bob Grauer is an Associate Professor in the Department of Computer Information Systems at the University of Miami, where he is a multiple winner of the Outstanding Teaching Award in the School of Business, most recently in 2009. He has written numerous COBOL texts and is the vision behind the Exploring Office series, with more than three million books in print. His work has been translated into three foreign languages and is used in all aspects of higher education at both national and international levels. Bob Grauer has consulted for several major corporations including IBM and American Express. He received his Ph.D. in operations research in 1972 from the Polytechnic Institute of Brooklyn.

CONTENTS

WINDOWS 7

CHAPTER 1 Getting Started with Windows 7 1

CASE STUDY: CEDAR COVE ELEMENTARY SCHOOL	1	
OBJECTIVES	1	
WINDOWS 7 FUNDAMENTALS	2	
Understanding the Desktop	2	
Managing Windows	12	
HANDS-ON EXERCISE 1:		
Windows 7 Fundamentals	16	
WINDOWS PROGRAMS AND SECURITY FEATURES	23	
Identifying Windows Accessories	23	
Working with Security Settings and Software	26	
HANDS-ON EXERCISE 2:		
Windows Programs and Security Features	31	
WINDOWS SEARCH AND HELP	35	
Performing a Search	35	
Getting Help	37	

HANDS-ON EXERCISE 3:	
Windows Search and Help	40
CHAPTER OBJECTIVES REVIEW	43
KEY TERMS	43
MULTIPLE CHOICE	44
PRACTICE EXERCISES	45
MID-LEVEL EXERCISES	48
CAPSTONE EXERCISE	49
BEYOND THE CLASSROOM	50
GLOSSARY	51
INDEX	53

CONTENTS

CHAPTER 1 Getting Started with Windows 7

GLOSSARY

INDEX

ACKNOWLEDGMENTS

The Exploring team would like to acknowledge and thank all the reviewers who helped us prepare for the Exploring Office 2010 revision by providing us with their invaluable comments, suggestions, and constructive criticism:

Allen Alexander
Delaware Technical & Community College

Andrea Marchese
Maritime College, State University of New York

Andrew Blitz
Broward College, Edison State College

Angela Clark
University of South Alabama

Astrid Todd
Guilford Technical Community College

Audrey Gillant
Maritime College, State University of New York

Barbara Stover
Marion Technical College

Barbara Tollinger
Sinclair Community College

Ben Brahim Taha
Auburn University

Beverly Amer
Northern Arizona University

Beverly Fite
Amarillo College

Bonnie Homan
San Francisco State University

Brad West
Sinclair Community College

Brian Powell
West Virginia University

Carol Buser
Owens Community College

Carol Roberts
University of Maine

Cathy Poyner
Truman State University

Charles Hodgson
Delgado Community College

Cheryl Hinds
Norfolk State University

Cindy Herbert
Metropolitan Community College–Longview

Dana Hooper
University of Alabama

Dana Johnson
North Dakota State University

Daniela Marghitu
Auburn University

David Noel
University of Central Oklahoma

David Pulis
Maritime College, State University of New York

David Thornton
Jacksonville State University

Dawn Medlin
Appalachian State University

Debby Keen
University of Kentucky

Debra Chapman
University of South Alabama

Derrick Huang
Florida Atlantic University

Diana Baran
Henry Ford Community College

Diane Cassidy
The University of North Carolina at Charlotte

Diane Smith
Henry Ford Community College

Don Danner
San Francisco State University

Don Hoggan
Solano College

Elaine Crable
Xavier University

Erhan Uskup
Houston Community College–Northwest

Erika Nadas
Wilbur Wright College

Floyd Winters
Manatee Community College

Frank Lucente
Westmoreland County Community College

G. Jan Wilms
Union University

Gail Cope
Sinclair Community College

Gary DeLorenzo
California University of Pennsylvania

Gary Garrison
Belmont University

Gerald Braun
Xavier University

Gladys Swindler
Fort Hays State University

Heith Hennel
Valencia Community College

Irene Joos
La Roche College

Iwona Rusin
Baker College; Davenport University

J. Roberto Guzman
San Diego Mesa College

Jan Wilms
Union University

Janet Bringhurst
Utah State University

Jim Chaffee
The University of Iowa Tippie College of Business

Joanne Lazirko
University of Wisconsin–Milwaukee

Jodi Milliner
Kansas State University

John Hollenbeck
Blue Ridge Community College

John Seydel
Arkansas State University

Judith A. Scheeren
Westmoreland County Community College

Judith Brown
The University of Memphis

Karen Priestly
Northern Virginia Community College

Karen Ravan
Spartanburg Community College

Kathleen Brenan
Ashland University

Ken Busbee
Houston Community College

Kent Foster
Winthrop University

Kevin Anderson
Solano Community College

Kim Wright
The University of Alabama

Kristen Hockman
University of Missouri–Columbia

Kristi Smith
Allegany College of Maryland

Laura McManamon
University of Dayton

Leanne Chun
Leeward Community College

Lee McClain
Western Washington University

Linda D. Collins
Mesa Community College

Linda Johnsonius
Murray State University

Linda Lau
Longwood University

Linda Theus
Jackson State Community College

Lisa Miller
University of Central Oklahoma

Lister Horn
Pensacola Junior College

Lixin Tao
Pace University

Loraine Miller
Cayuga Community College

Lori Kielty
Central Florida Community College

Lorna Wells
Salt Lake Community College

Lucy Parakhovnik (Parker)
California State University, Northridge

Marcia Welch
Highline Community College

Margaret McManus
Northwest Florida State College

Margaret Warrick
Allan Hancock College

Marilyn Hibbert
Salt Lake Community College

Mark Choman
Luzerne County Community College

Mary Duncan
University of Missouri – St. Louis

Melissa Nemeth
Indiana University Purdue University
Indianapolis

Melody Alexander
Ball State University

Michael Douglas
University of Arkansas at Little Rock

Michael Dunklebarger
Alamance Community College

Michael G. Skaff
College of the Sequoias

Michele Budnovitch
Pennsylvania College of Technology

Mike Jochen
East Stroudsburg University

Mike Scroggins
Missouri State University

Nanette Lareau
University of Arkansas Community College–
Morrilton

Pam Uhlenkamp
Iowa Central Community College

Patrick Smith
Marshall Community and Technical College

Paula Ruby
Arkansas State University

Peggy Burrus
Red Rocks Community College

Peter Ross
SUNY Albany

Philip H Nielson
Salt Lake Community College

Ralph Hooper
University of Alabama

Ranette Halverson
Midwestern State University

Richard Cacace
Pensacola Junior College

Robert Dušek
Northern Virginia Community College

Robert Sindt
Johnson County Community College

Rocky Belcher
Sinclair Community College

Roger Pick
University of Missouri at Kansas City

Ronnie Creel
Troy University

Rosalie Westerberg
Clover Park Technical College

Ruth Neal
Navarro College

Sandra Thomas
Troy University

Sophie Lee
California State University, Long Beach

Steven Schwarz
Raritan Valley Community College

Sue McCrory
Missouri State University

Susan Fuschetto
Cerritos College

Susan Medlin
UNC Charlotte

Suzan Spitzberg
Oakton Community College

Sven Aelterman
Troy University

Terri Holly
Indian River State College

Thomas Rienzo
Western Michigan University

Tina Johnson
Midwestern State University

Tommy Lu
Delaware Technical and Community College

Troy S. Cash
NorthWest Arkansas Community College

Vicki Robertson
Southwest Tennessee Community College

Weifeng Chen
California University of Pennsylvania

Wes Anthony
Houston Community College

William Ayen
University of Colorado at Colorado Springs

Wilma Andrews
Virginia Commonwealth University

Yvonne Galusha
University of Iowa

We'd also like to acknowledge the reviewers of previous editions of Exploring:

Aaron Schorr
Fashion Institute of Technology

Alan Moltz
Naugatuck Valley Technical Community College

Alicia Stonesifer
La Salle University

Allen Alexander
Delaware Tech & Community College

Alok Charturvedi
Purdue University

Amy Williams
Abraham Baldwin Agriculture College

Andrea Compton
St. Charles Community College

Annette Duvall
Central New Mexico Community College

Annie Brown
Hawaii Community College

Antonio Vargas
El Paso Community College

Barbara Cierny
Harper College

Barbara Hearn
Community College of Philadelphia

Barbara Meguro
University of Hawaii at Hilo

Barbara Sherman
Buffalo State College

Barbara Stover
Marion Technical College

Bette Pitts
South Plains College

Beverly Fite
Amarillo College

Bill Daley
University of Oregon

Bill Morse
DeVry Institute of Technology

Bill Wagner
Villanova

Bob McCloud
Sacred Heart University

Bonnie Homan
San Francisco State University

Brandi N. Guidry
University of Louisiana at Lafayette

Brian Powell
West Virginia University–Morgantown
Campus

Carl Farrell
Hawaii Pacific University

Carl M. Briggs
Indiana University School of Business

Carl Penzuil
Ithaca College

Carlotta Eaton
Radford University

Carole Bagley
University of St. Thomas

Carolyn DiLeo
Westchester Community College

Cassie Georgetti
Florida Technical College

Catherine Hain
Central New Mexico Community College

Charles Edwards
University of Texas of the Permian Basin

Cheryl Slavik
Computer Learning Services

Christine L. Moore
College of Charleston

Cody Copeland
Johnson County Community College

Connie Wells
Georgia State University

Dana Johnson
North Dakota State University

Dan Combellick
Scottsdale Community College

Daniela Marghitu
Auburn University

David B. Meinert
Southwest Missouri State University

David Barnes
Penn State Altoona

David Childress
Ashland Community College

David Douglas
University of Arkansas

David Langley
University of Oregon

David Law
Alfred State College

David Rinehard
Lansing Community College

David Weiner
University of San Francisco

Delores Pusins
Hillsborough Community College

Dennis Chalupa
Houston Baptist

Diane Stark
Phoenix College

Dianna Patterson
Texarkana College

Dianne Ross
University of Louisiana at Lafayette

Don Belle
Central Piedmont Community College

Douglas Cross
Clackamas Community College

Dr. Behrooz Saghafi
Chicago State University

Dr. Gladys Swindler
Fort Hays State University

Dr. Joe Teng
Barry University

Dr. Karen Nantz
Eastern Illinois University

Duane D. Lintner
Amarillo College

Elizabeth Edmiston
North Carolina Central University

Erhan Uskup
Houston Community College

Ernie Ivey
Polk Community College

Fred Hills
McClellan Community College

Freda Leonard
Delgado Community College

Gale E. Rand
College Misericordia

Gary R. Armstrong
Shippensburg University of Pennsylvania

Glenna Vanderhoof
Missouri State

Gregg Asher
Minnesota State University, Mankato

Hank Imus
San Diego Mesa College

Heidi Gentry-Kolen
Northwest Florida State College

Helen Stoloff
Hudson Valley Community College

Herach Safarian
College of the Canyons

Hong K. Sung
University of Central Oklahoma

Hyekyung Clark
Central New Mexico Community College

J Patrick Fenton
West Valley College

Jack Zeller
Kirkwood Community College

James Franck
College of St. Scholastica

James Gips
Boston College

Jana Carver
Amarillo College

Jane Cheng
Bloomfield College

Jane King
Everett Community College

Janis Cox
Tri-County Technical College

Janos T. Fustos
Metropolitan State College of Denver

Jean Kotsiovos
Kaplan University

Jeffrey A Hassett
University of Utah

Jennifer Pickle
Amarillo College

Jerry Chin
Southwest Missouri State University

Jerry Kolata
New England Institute of Technology

Jesse Day
South Plains College

Jill Chapnick
Florida International University

Jim Pepe
Bentley College

Jim Pruitt
Central Washington University

John Arehart
Longwood University

John Lee Reardon
University of Hawaii, Manoa

John Lesson
University of Central Florida

John Shepherd
Duquesne University

Joshua Mindel
San Francisco State University

Judith M. Fitspatrick
Gulf Coast Community College

Judith Rice
Santa Fe Community College

Judy Brown
The University of Memphis

Judy Dolan
Palomar College

Karen Tracey
Central Connecticut State University

Karen Wisniewski
County College of Morris

Karl Smart
Central Michigan University

Kathleen Brenan
Ashland University

Kathryn L. Hatch
University of Arizona

Kevin Pauli
University of Nebraska

Kim Montney
Kellogg Community College

Kimberly Chambers
Scottsdale Community College

Krista Lawrence
Delgado Community College

Krista Terry
Radford University

Lancie Anthony Affonso
College of Charleston

Larry S. Corman
Fort Lewis College

Laura McManamon
University of Dayton

Laura Reid
University of Western Ontario

Linda Johnsonius
Murray State University

Lisa Prince
Missouri State University

Lori Kelley
Madison Area Technical College

Lucy Parker
California State University, Northridge

Lynda Henrie
LDS Business College

Lynn Band
Middlesex Community College

Lynn Bowen
Valdosta Technical College

Malia Young
Utah State University

Margaret Thomas
Ohio University

Margie Martyn
Baldwin Wallace

Marguerite Nedreberg
Youngstown State University

Marianne Trudgeon
Fanshawe College

Marilyn Hibbert
Salt Lake Community College

Marilyn Salas
Scottsdale Community College

Marjean Lake
LDS Business College

Mark Olaveson
Brigham Young University

Martin Crossland
Southwest Missouri State University

Mary McKenry Percival
University of Miami

Meg McManus
Northwest Florida State College

Michael Hassett
Fort Hayes State University

Michael Stewardson
San Jacinto College–North

Midge Gerber
Southwestern Oklahoma State University

Mike Hearn
Community College of Philadelphia

Mike Kelly
Community College of Rhode Island

Mike Thomas
Indiana University School of Business

Mimi Duncan
University of Missouri–St. Louis

Minnie Proctor
Indian River Community College

Nancy Sardone
Seton Hall University

Pam Chapman
Waubonsee Community College

Patricia Joseph
Slippery Rock University

Patrick Hogan
Cape Fear Community College

Paul E. Daurelle
Western Piedmont Community
College

Paula F. Bell
Lock Haven University of Pennsylvania

Paulette Comet
Community College of Baltimore County,
Catonsville

Pratap Kotala
North Dakota State University

Ranette Halverson
Midwestern State University

Raymond Frost
Central Connecticut State University

Richard Albright
Goldey-Beacom College

Richard Blamer
John Carroll University

Richard Herschel
St. Joseph's University

Richard Hewer
Ferris State University

Robert Gordon
Hofstra University

Robert Marmelstein
East Stroudsburg University

Robert Spear
Prince George's Community College

Robert Stumbur
Northern Alberta Institute of Technology

Roberta I. Hollen
University of Central Oklahoma

Roland Moreira
South Plains College

Ron Murch
University of Calgary

Rory J. de Simone
University of Florida

Rose M. Laird
Northern Virginia Community College

Ruth Neal
Navarro College

Sally Visci
Lorain County Community College

Sandra M. Brown
Finger Lakes Community College

Sharon Mulroney
Mount Royal College

Shawna DePlonty
Sault College of Applied Arts and Technology

Stephen E. Lunce
Midwestern State University

Steve Schwarz
Raritan Valley Community College

Steven Choy
University of Calgary

Stuart P. Brian
Holy Family College

Susan Byrne
St. Clair College

Susan Fry
Boise State University

Suzan Spitzberg
Oakton Community College

Suzanne Tomlinson
Iowa State University

Thomas Setaro
Brookdale Community College

Todd McLeod
Fresno City College

Vernon Griffin
Austin Community College

Vickie Pickett
Midland College

Vipul Gupta
St. Joseph's University

Vivek Shah
Texas State University–San Marcos

Wei-Lun Chuang
Utah State University

William Dorin
Indiana University Northwest

Finally, we'd like to extend our thanks to the Exploring 2010 technical editors:

Janet Pickard

Janice Snyder

Joyce Nielsen

Julie Boyles

PREFACE

The Exploring Series

Exploring is Pearson's most demanding Office Application series, requiring students to think beyond the skills. For Office 2007, Exploring underwent the most extensive changes in its history, so that the series truly moves today's student "beyond the point and click."

The goal of Exploring has always been to teach more than just the steps to accomplish a task—the series provides the theoretical foundation necessary for students to understand when and why to apply a skill. This way, students achieve a deeper understanding of the Office applications.

Today's students are changing and Exploring is evolving with them. Pearson traveled to college campuses across the country and spoke directly with students to determine how they study and prepare for class. We also spoke with hundreds of professors about the best ways to administer materials to such a diverse body of students.

Here Is What We Learned

Students go to college now with a different set of skills than they did five years ago. They are very tech savvy, but not necessarily Office savvy. Exploring moves students beyond the basics of the software at a faster pace, without sacrificing coverage of the fundamental skills that every student needs to know. This ensures that students will be engaged from page 1.

Students read, prepare, and study differently than they used to. Students use their textbook like a tool—they want to easily identify what they need to know and learn it efficiently. Key features such as objective mapping, pull quotes, and key terms in the margins bring students into the content and make the text easy to use.

Students are very goal-oriented. They want a good grade now and they want to be successful in their future careers. With this in mind, we used motivating case studies woven into the chapter to aid students in learning now and to show the relevance of the skills to their future careers.

Moving Students Beyond the Point and Click

Exploring students will be engaged, achieve a higher level of understanding, and successfully complete this course to go on to be successful in their careers. In addition to the experience and expertise of the series creator and author Robert T. Grauer, we have assembled a tremendously talented team of co-authors to take the reins with this revision. Each of them is equally dedicated to continuing the Exploring mission of **moving students beyond the point and click**.

Key Features of Exploring Getting Started with Windows 7

- **White Pages/Yellow Pages** clearly distinguish the theory (white pages) from the skills covered in the Hands-On Exercises (yellow pages) so students always know what they are supposed to be doing.

- **Objective Mapping** enables students to skip the skills and concepts they know, and quickly find those they don't, by scanning the chapter opener page for the page numbers of the material they need.

- **Pull Quotes** entice students into the theory by highlighting the most interesting points.

- **Case Study** presents a scenario for the chapter, creating a story that ties the Hands-On Exercises together.

- **Set-Up Video** introduces the chapter's Case Study to generate student interest and attention.

- **Key Terms** are defined in the margins to ensure student comprehension.

- **End of Chapter Exercises** offer instructors several options for assessment. Each chapter has approximately 12–15 exercises ranging from multiple choice questions to open-ended projects.

- **Enhanced Mid-Level Exercises** include a Creative Case, which allows students some flexibility and creativity, not being bound by a definitive solution, and Discover Steps, which encourage students to use Help or problem-solve to accomplish a task.

Instructor Resources

The Instructor's Resource Center, available at www.pearsonhighered.com includes the following:

- **Capstone Production Tests** allow instructors to assess all of the skills covered in a chapter with a single project.

- **Rubrics** for Mid-Level Creative Cases and Beyond the Classroom Cases in Microsoft® Word format enable instructors to customize the assignments for their classes.

- **PowerPoint® Presentations** with notes for each chapter are included for online students.

- **Lesson Plans** provide a detailed blueprint for an instructor to achieve chapter learning objectives and outcomes.

- **Objectives List** maps chapter objectives to Hands-On Exercises and End-of-Chapter Exercises.

- **Student Data Files**

- **Solution Files**

- **Annotated Solution Files**

- **Multiple Choice Answer Key**

- **Complete Test Bank**

- **Instructor Reference Cards** for each chapter that include a:
  - **Concept Summary** that outlines the KEY objectives to cover in class with tips on where students get stuck as well as how to get them un-stuck. This helps bridge the gap between the instructor and student when discussing more difficult topics.
  - **Scripted Lecture** which provides instructors with a lecture outline that mirrors the Hands-On Exercises in the chapter.

Online Course Cartridges

Flexible, robust and customizable content is available for all major online course platforms that include everything instructors need in one place. Please contact your Sales Representative for information on accessing course cartridges for WebCT, Blackboard, or CourseCompass.

Student Resources

Prentice Hall's Companion Web Site

www.pearsonhighered.com/exploring offers expanded IT resources and downloadable supplements. Students can find the following self-study tools for each chapter:

- Online Study Guide

- Chapter Objectives

- Glossary

- Chapter Objectives Review

- Web Resources

- Student Data Files

- Set-Up Video

Senior Vice President, Editorial and Marketing: Patrick F. Boles
Associate Editor: Ana Díaz-Caneja
Development Editor: Christina Martin
Marketing Manager: Jack Cooney
Operations Manager: Eric M. Kenney
Production Manager: Jennifer Berry
Rights Manager: Jillian Santos
Art Director: Renée Sartell
Cover Designers: Blair Brown and Kisten Kiley

Cover Art: Jerry Driendl/Getty Images, Inc.; Steve Bloom/Getty Images, Inc.; "Cheetah" courtesy of Marvin Mattelson/Getty Images; "Tabs" courtesy of Andrey Prokhorov/iStockphoto; "Open Doors" courtesy of Spectral-Design/iStockphoto; "Compass" courtesy of Laurent Hamels/Getty Images; "Fortune Teller" courtesy of Ingvald Kaldhussaeter/iStockphoto; "Ladder of Success" courtesy of iStockphoto; "Global Communication in Blue" courtesy of iStockphoto.

This special edition published in cooperation with Pearson Learning Solutions.

Printed in the United States of America.

Please visit our web site at *www.pearsoncustom.com*

Attention bookstores: For permission to return any unsold stock, contact us at *pe-uscustomreturns@pearson.com*.

Pearson Learning Solutions, 501 Boylston Street, Suite 900, Boston, MA 02116
A Pearson Education Company
www.pearsoned.com

ISBN 10: 0-558-46343-6
ISBN 13: 978-0-558-46343-4

Attention Students

How to Find Your Student Data Files

Some projects in this book begin from a student data file that has already been started for you. The student data files can be accessed from the Custom PHIT Web site, www.pearsoncustom.com/customphit/datafiles

Because this is a custom book, student data file names are not always consistent with chapter numbers in your book's Table of Contents. Be sure that any student data file that you use exactly matches the file name cited in the chapter.

Files from www.pearsoncustom.com/customphit/datafiles

1 Decide where you want to store your student data files.

- If you are storing on the hard drive of your computer or on a network drive, you may want create a folder with an appropriate name on that drive.

- If you are storing on a removable storage device such as a USB flash drive, Zip® disk, or floppy disk, insert the device now.

2 From your Web browser, go to **www.pearsoncustom.com/customphit/datafiles**

3 Select the series and the book that is the source of the files that you need.

4 From the list of the available resources, point to the link for the files you need, and then click the active link.

5 In the displayed dialog box, click the command to **Save** and then click **OK**.

6 In the displayed dialog box, navigate to the location where you decided to store your files—either in a folder on your hard drive or network drive, or on your removable storage device.

7 Click **Save** to begin the downloading process. When complete you can close your browser.

8 As specifically directed in each project, navigate to the location where you have stored the student data files and then save and rename the file according to the instructions in the project.

WINDOWS 7

1 GETTING STARTED WITH WINDOWS 7

CASE STUDY | Cedar Cove Elementary School

A good friend recently graduated with a degree in Elementary Education and is excited to begin her first job as a fifth-grade teacher at Cedar Cove Elementary School. The school has a computer lab for all students as well as a computer system in each classroom. The computers were acquired through a state technology grant so they are new models running Windows 7. Your friend's lesson plans must include a unit on operating system basics and an introduction to application software. Because you have a degree in Computer Information Systems, she has called on you for assistance with the lesson plans. She also hopes you will occasionally visit her classroom to help present the material.

The elementary school is located in a low-income area of the city, so you cannot assume that all students have been exposed to computers at home, especially to those configured with Windows 7. Your material will need to include very basic instruction in Windows 7, along with a general overview of application software. You will probably focus on application software that is included with Windows 7, including WordPad, Paint, and Calculator. Your friend's lesson plans must be completed right away, so you are on a short timeline but are excited about helping students learn!

OBJECTIVES AFTER YOU READ THIS CHAPTER, YOU WILL BE ABLE TO:

1. Understand the desktop
2. Manage windows
3. Identify Windows accessories
4. Work with security settings and software
5. Perform a search
6. Get help

From Chapter 1 of *Exploring Getting Started with Windows 7*, First Edition, Robert T. Grauer, Lynn Hogan and Mary Anne Poatsy.

Windows 7 Fundamentals

Computer activities that you enjoy might include e-mail, games, social networking, and digital photo management. If you have a computer at work, you probably use such software as spreadsheet, database, word processing, and other job-specific applications. Those applications are necessary for your enjoyment or career, but they would not be possible without an *operating system*. The operating system is software that directs such computer activities as checking all components, managing system resources, and communicating with application software.

> Windows 7 is a Microsoft operating system produced in 2009 and available on most new microcomputer systems.

Windows 7 is a Microsoft operating system produced in 2009 and available on most new *microcomputer* systems. Because you are likely to encounter Windows 7 on computers at school, work, and home, it is well worth your time to explore it and learn to appreciate its computer management and security features. In this section, you will explore the desktop and its components, including the Start menu and taskbar. You will also learn to customize the desktop with a background and color scheme of your choice.

An **operating system** is software that directs computer activities such as recognizing keyboard input, sending output to a display, and keeping track of files and folders.

Understanding the Desktop

The **desktop** is the screen that displays when you turn on a computer. It contains icons and a taskbar.

A **window** is an onscreen rectangular area representing a program or system resource, or data.

The *desktop* is the display that you see after you turn on a computer and respond to any username and password prompts. The Windows 7 desktop includes components that enable you to access system resources, work with software, and manage files and folders. It is called a *desktop* because it serves the purpose of a desk, on which you can manage tasks and complete paperwork. Just as you can work with multiple projects on a desk, you can work with several software applications, each occupying a *window*, or area of space, on the desktop.

Identify Desktop Components

An **icon** is a small picture on the desktop representing a program, file, folder, or other item.

One of the first things that you will notice about the desktop is the presence of a few small pictures, each with a description underneath. Those pictures, or *icons*, represent programs, files, folders, or other items related to your computer. The desktop that you see on your home computer might differ from the one that you use at school or work because each computer has a unique configuration of installed programs and files. Invariably, most desktops contain one or more icons such as the one shown in Figure 1. You can easily add and remove

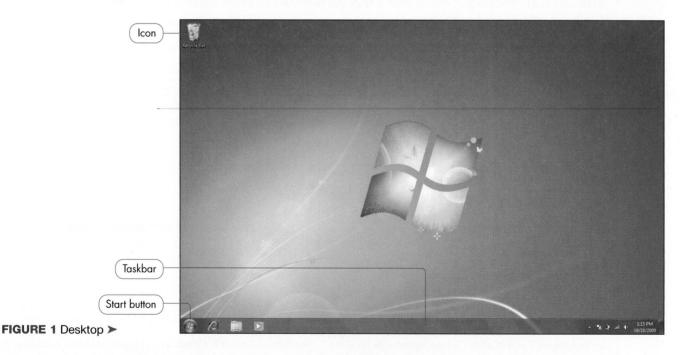

Icon

Taskbar

Start button

FIGURE 1 Desktop ➤

icons so that the desktop includes only those items that are important to you or that you access often. You can even include desktop folders in which you can organize files and programs.

As you work with a computer, you will find that you access some programs, or software, more often than others. Instead of searching for the program on a program list, you will find it convenient to add a program icon to the desktop. The icon is not actually the program, but a link to the program, called a *shortcut*. Such shortcut icons are identified by a small arrow in the bottom left corner of the icon. Figure 2 shows a shortcut icon. A computer provides a large amount of storage space, some of which you might use to house files, such as documents, worksheets, and digital photos related to particular projects or work-related activities. Because the desktop is so convenient to access, you could create a folder, identified by a folder icon, on the desktop to organize such files. See the folder icon in Figure 2. If you save files to the desktop, you should organize them in desktop folders. That way, the desktop will not become too cluttered and you can easily find related files later. Keep in mind that just as you strive to keep a desk relatively clear, you will also want to maintain order on the Windows desktop.

A **shortcut** is a pointer, or link, to a program or computer resource.

Folder icon

Shortcut icon

FIGURE 2 Icons ➤

You can easily add icons to the desktop, but the way in which you add an icon depends on the icon's purpose.

- **To add a program shortcut to the desktop**, you must first locate the program. Most often, you can simply click the Start button (located in the bottom left corner of the desktop). Point to All Programs. Navigate the menu to display the program, but do not open it. Instead, right-click and drag the program name to the desktop. Release the mouse button. Click Create shortcuts here.
- **To add a folder to the desktop**, right-click an empty area of the desktop. Point to New and click Folder. Type a folder name and press Enter.

You can also delete and rename icons, as described below.

- **To delete an icon**, right-click the icon and click Delete. Respond affirmatively if asked whether to place the icon in the Recycle Bin. Remember that deleting a program shortcut icon does not remove, or uninstall, the program itself. You simply remove the desktop pointer (shortcut) to the program.
- **To rename an icon**, right-click the icon and click Rename. Type the new name and press Enter.

TIP Auto Arrange Icons

A desktop can easily become cluttered and disorganized. To avoid clutter, make sure that you maintain only desktop icons that are accessed often or that are important to keep handy. To neatly organize the desktop, you can auto arrange the icons. Right-click an empty area of the desktop, point to View, and click Auto arrange icons (unless Auto arrange icons already has a checkmark). Icons are maintained in straight columns and cannot be moved out of line.

A **gadget** is a desktop item that represents such items as games or puzzles, or constantly changing data, such as a clock or a calendar. Gadgets can be selected or downloaded and opened on the desktop.

Another item that can be placed on the desktop is a desktop *gadget*. A gadget represents data that is constantly changing, or an item such as a game or puzzle. Although some gadgets are available when you install Windows 7, you can add additional gadgets from the Microsoft Windows Web site. To view the gadgets that are available within Windows, right-click an empty area of the desktop and click Gadgets. The gallery shown in Figure 3 displays. Double-click a gadget to place it on the desktop. Click Get more gadgets online to download others. To remove a gadget from the desktop, right-click the gadget and click Close gadget.

FIGURE 3 Gadgets Gallery ➤

By default, gadgets are grouped together on the right side of the desktop. By changing a few settings, you can resize gadgets, cause them to always appear on top of any open windows, adjust the opacity level, and move them. All of these options are available when you right-click a gadget on the desktop.

Explore the Taskbar

You can have several projects, papers, and other items on a desk. In fact, you can have so many things on a desk that it becomes difficult to sort through them all. Similarly, you can have several windows, or applications, open on a computer desktop at one time. Unlike a desk, however, the Windows

The Windows desktop provides a tool for keeping track of open computer projects—the taskbar.

The **taskbar** is the horizontal bar at the bottom of the desktop that enables you to move among open windows and provides access to system resources.

The **Start button**, located on the left side of the taskbar, is the place to begin when you want to open programs, get help, adjust computer settings, access system resources, or even shut down a computer.

The **Notification area**, on the right side of the taskbar, displays icons for background programs and system resources. It also provides status information in pop-up windows.

desktop provides a tool for keeping track of open computer projects—the *taskbar*. The taskbar is a long horizontal bar located at the bottom of the desktop. The taskbar is the location of the *Start button*, toolbars, open window buttons, and the *Notification area.*

When you open a program or work with a file, the item will display in a window on the desktop. It is not unusual to have several windows open at one time. When that happens, the windows sometimes overlap, making it difficult to see what is underneath or to remember what you have open. The taskbar simplifies the task of keeping track of the desktop. Every open window has a corresponding icon on the taskbar. Icons often represent programs, such as Excel and Word. To move from one window to another, simply click the taskbar icon representing the window. It works much like shifting paper on a desk but is easier. Figure 4 shows two windows open on the desktop, with corresponding taskbar program icons. Although several windows can be open at one time, only one is active (in front of other windows).

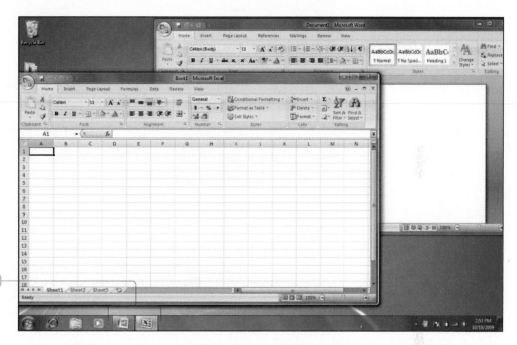

Program icons

FIGURE 4 Program Icons on the Taskbar ➤

Aero Peek provides a preview of an open window without requiring you to click away from the window that you are currently working on. Place the mouse pointer over any icon that represents an open window to view its contents.

Windows 7 taskbar icons are large and unlabeled, unlike icons found in earlier Windows versions. The size and simplicity gives a clean uncluttered feel to the taskbar. Even if you have multiple files open for one icon, such as when you have several word processing documents open, you will see only one program icon. If several programs are open, you will see a taskbar icon for each open window. To get a sneak preview of any open window, even if it is obscured by another, place the mouse pointer over the program's icon on the taskbar. The resulting preview is called *Aero Peek*. Place the mouse pointer over the thumbnail (previewed window), without clicking, to temporarily view the window in full size. When you move the mouse pointer away, the active window reappears. If you click the thumbnail (window preview) you will switch to the previewed window. See Figure 5 for an example of Aero Peek.

Aero Peek preview

FIGURE 5 Aero Peek ➤

The **Start menu** is a list of programs, folders, and utilities that displays when you click the Start button.

When you click the Start button, you will see the *Start menu,* as shown in Figure 6. As its name implies, the Start menu is the place to begin when you want to open programs, get help, adjust computer settings, access system resources, or even shut down your computer. The Start menu is comprised of three areas. The *left pane* displays a short list of commonly accessed programs on your computer. When you point to All Programs, you will see a more complete list of programs. The *right pane* provides access to system folders, such as Documents, Pictures, and Music. It also enables you to adjust system settings, log off a user account, shut down the computer, and get help. The *Search box,* located at the bottom of the left side of the Start menu (see Figure 6), is where you can type keywords of an item you are looking for, such as a file or folder. You will explore the topic of searching later in this chapter.

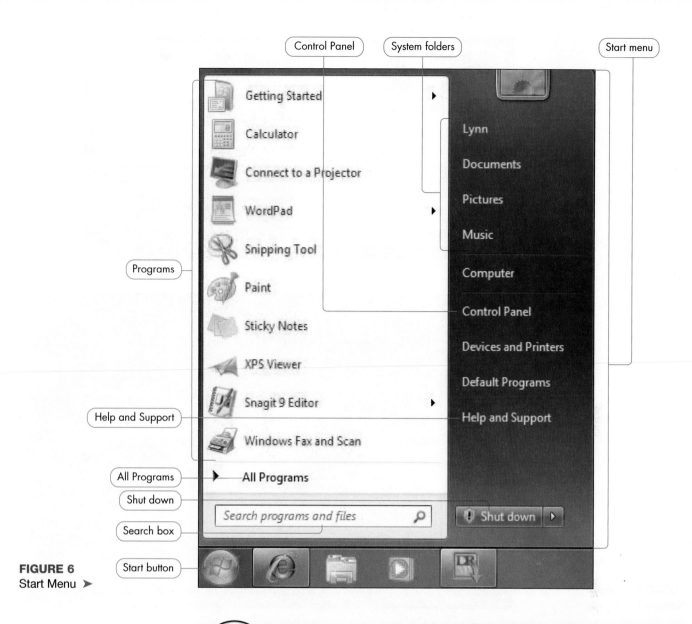

Control Panel System folders Start menu

Getting Started

Calculator

Connect to a Projector

WordPad

Snipping Tool

Programs

Paint

Sticky Notes

XPS Viewer

Snagit 9 Editor

Help and Support

Windows Fax and Scan

All Programs

Shut down

Search box

Start button

Lynn

Documents

Pictures

Music

Computer

Control Panel

Devices and Printers

Default Programs

Help and Support

All Programs

Search programs and files

Shut down

FIGURE 6
Start Menu ➤

TIP Hide the Taskbar

Although it is very helpful, the taskbar can occupy space on your work area that you need. To temporarily hide the taskbar, right-click an empty area of the taskbar. Click Properties. In the Taskbar appearance area of the Taskbar and Start Menu Properties window, click to select Auto-hide the taskbar, and then click OK. The taskbar immediately disappears. When you move the mouse pointer to the previous location of the taskbar, it will appear, but only until you move the mouse pointer away. To return the taskbar to view, reverse the process described above, clicking to deselect Auto-hide the taskbar.

A **toolbar** is an area of items that you can select, usually displayed on the taskbar or within an application.

The taskbar is a convenient place to display *toolbars*, which provide shortcuts to Web resources and enable you to quickly move to a specified address. Specifically the Links and Address toolbars are handy additions to the taskbar but are not automatically displayed. To see a list of available toolbars, right-click an empty part of the taskbar and point to Toolbars. See Figure 7 for an example of a toolbar list. Click any item in the list to add or remove it. If you see a checkmark beside a toolbar, the toolbar is already open on the taskbar. Figure 8 shows a taskbar that includes an Address toolbar.

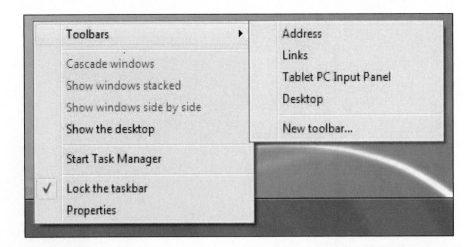

FIGURE 7 Taskbar
Toolbar List ➤

FIGURE 8 Toolbar
Example ➤

When you **pin** an item, it becomes a permanent part of the taskbar, accessible with a single click.

A **Jump List** is a list of actions or resources associated with an open window button or pinned item on the taskbar.

You can place, or *pin*, icons of frequently used programs on the taskbar for quick access later. When you pin a program, the program icon becomes a permanent part of the taskbar, as shown in Figure 9. You can then open the program by single-clicking its icon. If the program that you want to pin is not already open, click Start, browse to the program name, right-click the name, and click Pin to Taskbar. If the program that you want to pin is already open, right-click the program icon on the taskbar to open its *Jump List* (see Figure 9). Click Pin this program to taskbar. A Jump List is a list of shortcuts to pinned items, most often simply the program name, an option to pin or unpin an item, and a close option.

Getting Started with Windows 7

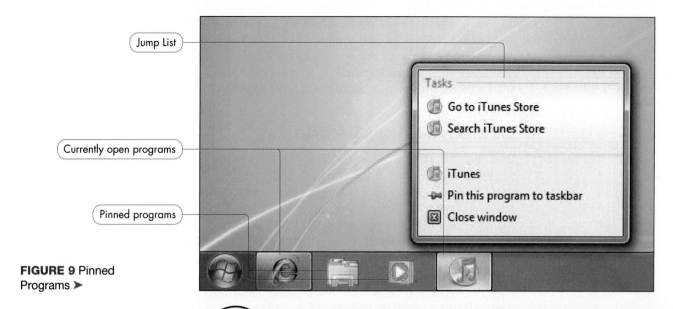

FIGURE 9 Pinned Programs ➤

Jump List

Currently open programs

Pinned programs

TIP Pin Items to the Start Menu

Just as you can pin programs to the taskbar, you can pin items to the Start menu. When you pin a program to the Start menu, it becomes a permanent selection on the left side of the Start menu. A pinned program always shows on the Start menu so that you can find the program easily and open it with a single click. To pin a program, locate its name on the Start menu, right-click it, and click Pin to Start Menu. You can pin a program from the Start menu to both the Start menu and the taskbar, but you cannot pin a program from the taskbar to the Start menu.

A major purpose of the Notification area is providing important status information that appears in a pop-up window when you click the Action Center icon.

You will find the Notification area (see Figure 10) on the right side of the taskbar. It displays icons for programs running in the background, such as a virus scanner, and provides access to such system activities as managing wireless networks and adjusting volume. A major purpose of the Notification area is to provide important status information that appears in a pop-up window when you click the Action Center icon. Status information could include the detection of new devices, the availability of software updates,

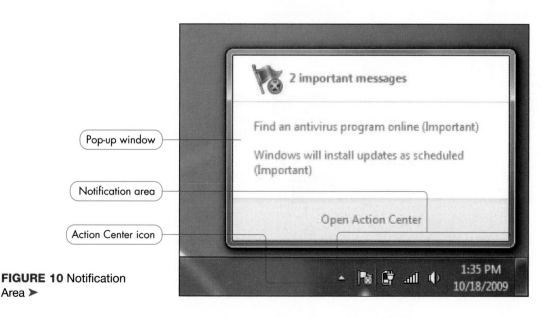

FIGURE 10 Notification Area ➤

Pop-up window

Notification area

Action Center icon

The **Action Center** monitors maintenance and security settings, providing alerts when necessary.

or recommended maintenance and security tasks. An example of a pop-up notification is given in Figure 10. If the notification is of a recommended update or maintenance task, you can click the message to perform the recommended task. If you see an *Action Center* icon associated with the notification, click it to open the Action Center for additional details. You will find more information about the Action Center later in this chapter.

Customize the Desktop

Each time you turn on your computer, you see the desktop. For a little variety you can customize the desktop with a different background or color theme. You can even include a slide show of favorite photos to display when your computer is idle. Customizing the desktop can be fun and creative. Windows 7 provides a wide selection of background and color choices.

A **screen saver** is a series of moving images that appears on the desktop when a computer has been idle for a specified period of time.

To change the desktop background, add moving images, or change the color theme, right-click an empty area of the desktop and click Personalize. Make a selection from those shown in Figure 11. If you choose to change the background, click Desktop Background (see Figure 11). Then select or confirm the picture location (see Figure 12). You can choose from built-in categories such as Windows Desktop Backgrounds, or you can browse for a folder containing your personal pictures. If you select Windows Desktop Backgrounds, you can select from several categories (nature, architecture, etc.). Click Window Color (see Figure 11) to change the color of window borders, the Start menu, and the taskbar. You can also select a *screen saver* (see Figure 11). A screen saver is a moving series of pictures or images that appears when your computer has been idle for a specified period of time. You might use a screen saver for privacy, so that when you are away from your desk, the display is obscured by the moving images. Figure 13 shows the Screen Saver Settings dialog box from which you can select a screen saver and adjust settings. Settings include how long the computer must be idle before a screen saver is displayed, as well as the option to require a log on before the screen saver disappears. Click Save Changes (see Figure 12) after making any of the above selections or Cancel to ignore changes. Close any open windows.

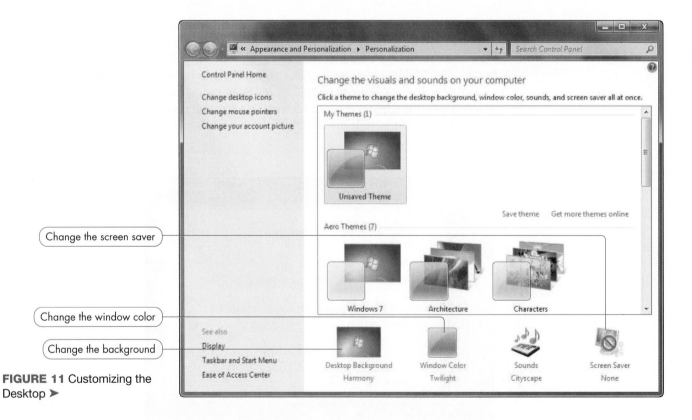

FIGURE 11 Customizing the Desktop ➤

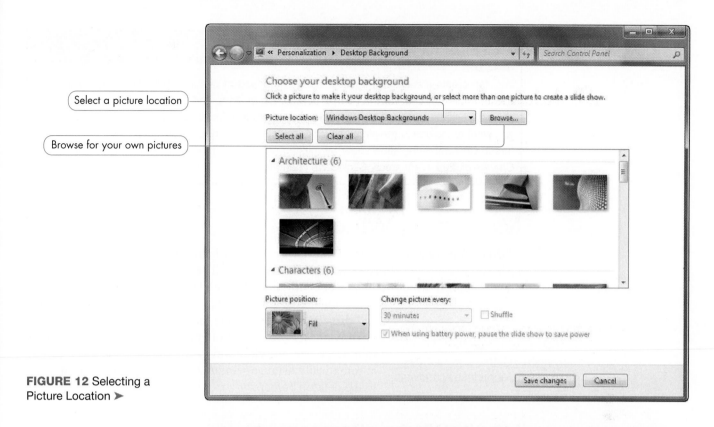

Select a picture location

Browse for your own pictures

FIGURE 12 Selecting a
Picture Location ➤

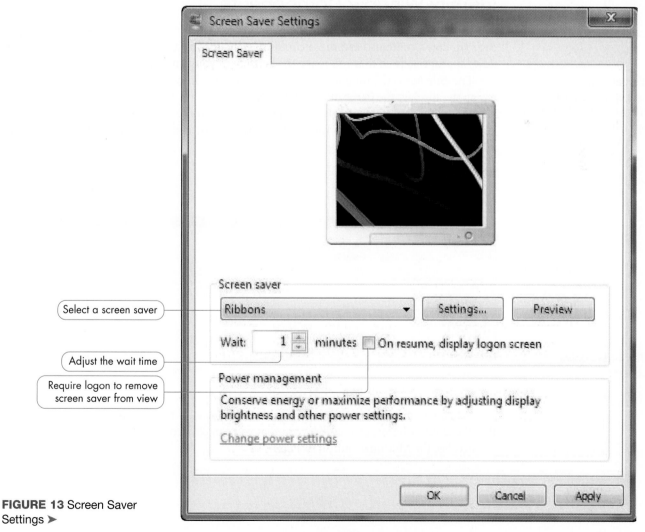

Select a screen saver

Adjust the wait time

Require logon to remove
screen saver from view

FIGURE 13 Screen Saver
Settings ➤

Managing Windows

When you open a program, file, or folder, it opens in a window. You can have many windows open at the same time. If that is the case, the windows will begin to overlap and obscure each other. Although Windows 7 can work with multiple open windows within its multitasking environment, you might find it difficult to manage the windows and projects effectively. Using the taskbar, you can move among open windows with ease, but you will also need to know how to move, resize, and close windows. Windows 7 makes it easy to automatically arrange windows, even snapping them quickly to the desktop borders.

> Using the taskbar, you can move among open windows with ease, but you will also need to know how to move, resize, and close windows.

Identify Window Components

All windows share common elements including a title bar and control buttons. Although each window's contents vary, those common elements make it easy for you to manage windows appropriately so that you make the best use of your time and computer resources.

> The **title bar** is the long bar at the top of each open window, containing the file or folder name and the program name.

The *title bar* is the long bar at the top of each window, as shown in Figure 14. The title bar always displays the name of the file and the program (or the name of the folder if you are viewing folder contents). Control buttons are found on the right side of the title bar. Those control buttons enable you to minimize, maximize (or restore down), and close any open window.

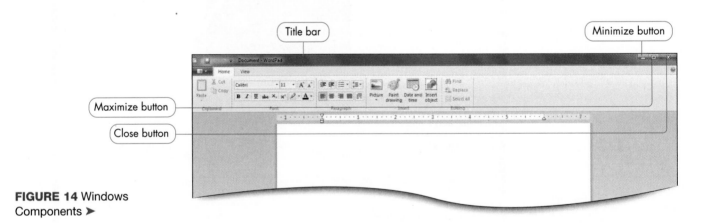

FIGURE 14 Windows Components ➤

When you minimize a window, you hide it from view but do not close it. That means that the window becomes a taskbar icon that you can click to return the window to its original size. See the Minimize button in Figure 14.

The middle control button shares two functions depending on the current size of the window. One is to maximize a window and one is to restore down to a smaller size. If a window is less than full size, click the middle button to maximize the window so that it occupies the entire desktop. The Maximize button looks like a small box. The restore down button appears as two overlapped boxes. The middle button in Figure 14 is a Maximize button. You can also maximize or restore down a window by double-clicking the title bar of the open window.

TIP Maximize a Window and Expand a Window Vertically

You can quickly maximize a window by clicking and dragging the title bar to the top of the desktop. The window immediately becomes full sized. To expand a window vertically without changing the window's width, click and drag a top or bottom border to the corresponding top or bottom edge of the desktop. When you place the mouse pointer on a border of a window, the pointer assumes the shape of a double-headed arrow. Only then should you click and drag the window to the top or bottom edge of the desktop. Release the mouse button to expand the window vertically.

The button on the far right side of the title bar is used to close a window. It is always displayed as an X. When you close a window, you remove the file or program from memory. If you have not saved a file that you are closing, Windows 7 will prompt you to save it before closing.

Work with Windows

It is sometimes necessary to move or resize a window. If multiple windows are open, you will need to know how to switch between windows and how to rearrange them. Windows 7 provides easy ways to select among windows, including the Aero Flip 3D experience.

If a window is obscuring something that you need to see, you can move or resize the window to reveal what is behind.

If a window is obscuring something that you need to see, you can move or resize the window to reveal what is behind. You can only move or resize a window that is not maximized. To move a window, click and drag the title bar. To resize a window, place the mouse pointer on a border of the window. The pointer will become a double-headed arrow. Click and drag to make the window larger or smaller. If the pointer is on a corner of the window, forming a diagonal double-headed arrow, you can resize two adjacent sides of the window at once by clicking and dragging.

You can also use the keyboard to switch to another window. To cycle through all open windows, stopping at any one, hold down Alt on the keyboard and repeatedly press Tab. Release Alt when you see the window that you want to display. *Aero Flip 3D* arranges all open windows in a three-dimensional stack that you can quickly flip through. Figure 15 shows a sample Aero Flip 3D stack. Hold down the Windows logo key and press Tab to cycle through open windows. Release the Windows logo key to stop on any window. You can also click any window in the stack to display it.

Aero Flip 3D is a feature that shows windows in a rotating 3D stack so that you can select a window.

Given what you know about resizing and moving windows, you can rearrange windows to suit your purposes. You can minimize or close those that are not necessary, returning to them later. Even so, you might prefer to let Windows 7 arrange your windows automatically. Windows 7 can arrange windows in a cascading fashion, vertically stacked, or side by side. If multiple windows are open on the desktop, right-click an empty part of the taskbar. Click Cascade windows, Show windows stacked, or Show windows side by side.

Snap arranges windows automatically along the left and right sides of the desktop.

Snap is a Windows 7 feature that will automatically place a window on the side of the desktop, resulting in a well-ordered arrangement of windows. Simply click and drag the title

FIGURE 15 Aero Flip 3D Stack ➤

bar of a window to the left or right side of the desktop until an outline of the window appears. Release the mouse button. Do the same with another window.

Earlier in this section, you learned that Aero Peek is a Windows 7 feature that enables you to preview open windows, switching to them if you like. Another function of Aero Peek is to provide a quick way to show the desktop without actually removing or minimizing windows. Simply point to the Show desktop button, shown in Figure 16. A quick way to show the desktop without actually removing or minimizing windows is to point to the Show desktop button, shown in Figure 16. If you simply want to see the desktop temporarily, do not click the Show desktop button—just point to it; the desktop displays. When you move away from the button, windows reappear as they were previously. If you do want to minimize all open windows, click the Show desktop button. Click the button again to return the windows to view (or click the corresponding icons on the taskbar).

The preceding discussion of windows focused on those windows that represent programs, files, or folders. Those could be considered standard windows. A **_dialog box_** is a special window that displays when an operation requires confirmation or additional

A **dialog box** is a special window that opens when you are accomplishing a specific task and when your confirmation or interaction is required.

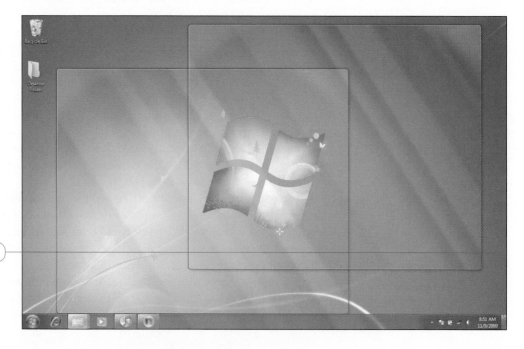

Show desktop button

FIGURE 16 Showing the Desktop ➤

information. Figure 17 shows a typical dialog box. By responding to areas of the dialog box, you can indicate how you want an operation to occur and how the program should behave. In effect, a dialog box asks for interaction with you before completing a procedure. You cannot minimize or maximize a dialog box, but you can move it. You can close it or make selections, get help by clicking the ? button (if present), and click the OK command button (or Cancel if you want to ignore any selections you might have made). Print dialog box selections are shown in Figure 17 and summarized below.

- *Option buttons* indicate mutually exclusive choices, one of which *must* be chosen, such as the page range. In this example, you can print all pages, the selection (if it is available), the current page, or a specific set of pages (such as pages 1–4), but you must choose *one and only one* option. When you select an option, any previously selected option is deselected.
- A *text box*, such as the one shown beside the *Pages* option in Figure 17, enables you to enter specific information. In this case, you could type 1–5 in the text box if you wanted only the first five pages to print.
- A *spin arrow* is a common component of a dialog box, providing a quick method of increasing or decreasing a setting. For example, clicking the spin arrow (or spinner) beside *Number of copies* enables you to increase or decrease the number of copies of the document to print.
- *Check boxes* are used instead of option buttons if the choices are not mutually exclusive. You can select or clear options by clicking the appropriate check box, which toggles the operation on and off. In Figure 17, you can select either or both options of printing to a file or using manual duplex. Unlike an option button, check boxes enable you to make several selections at the same time.
- A *list box* displays some or all of the available choices, any of which can be selected by clicking the list item. For example, you can choose from several print options, including printing all pages, or only odd or even pages.
- All dialog boxes also contain one or more *command buttons* that provide options to either accept or cancel your selections. The OK button, for example, initiates the printing process shown in Figure 17. The Cancel button does just the opposite and ignores (cancels) any changes made to the settings, closing the dialog box.

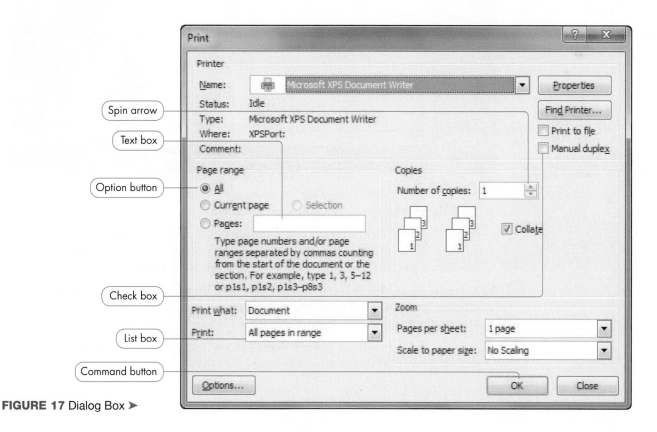

FIGURE 17 Dialog Box ➤

HANDS-ON EXERCISES

1 Windows 7 Fundamentals

Tomorrow you will meet with the Cedar Cove class to present an introduction to Windows 7. There is only one computer in the classroom, connected to a projector. You plan to demonstrate a few basics of working with the operating system including managing windows, adding gadgets, and working with the taskbar and Start menu. Above all, you want to keep it simple so that you encourage class enthusiasm. You have prepared a script that you plan to follow and you will practice it in the steps that follow.

Skills covered: Open, Resize, Move, and Close a Window • Manage Multiple Windows, Arrange Windows Automatically, Arrange Windows Using *Snap* • Add and Remove Gadgets, Add Shortcuts to the Desktop, Identify Icons • Explore the Start Menu, Pin Items to the Start Menu, Customize the Taskbar, Pin Items to the Taskbar • Change the Desktop Background and Screen Saver.

STEP 1 ▶ OPEN, RESIZE, MOVE, AND CLOSE A WINDOW

Before the students can work with software, they must learn to work with windows. Specifically, they must understand that software and other system settings will display in a window and they must become comfortable opening, closing, resizing, and moving windows. You will stress the importance of the desktop as the location of all windows. Refer to Figure 18 as you complete Step 1.

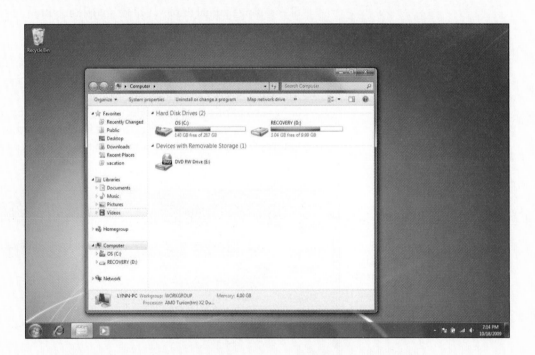

FIGURE 18 Computer Window ➤

a. Click the **Start button**. Click **Computer** in the right pane.

You have opened the Computer window, giving a summary of your computer's disk configuration. The window contents are not important at this time; you are interested in it only as an example of a window that you can use to demonstrate Windows basics.

b. Compare the window to that shown in Figure 18. If the window already fills the desktop, click the **Restore Down button** (the middle button) to restore the window to a smaller size. If it is less than full size, leave it as is.

c. Place the mouse pointer on a corner of the window. The pointer should appear as a double-headed arrow. Click and drag to make the window slightly smaller.

d. Place the mouse pointer on the title bar of the window. Click and drag to move it to another location on the desktop.

e. Place the mouse pointer on the top border of the window. Click and drag to make the window slightly larger.

f. Click the **Close button** (shown as an X) in the top right corner of the window to close it.

STEP 2 ▶ **MANAGE MULTIPLE WINDOWS, ARRANGE WINDOWS AUTOMATICALLY, ARRANGE WINDOWS USING *SNAP***

Because there will be occasions when several windows are open simultaneously, students must learn to arrange them. You will show them various ways that Windows 7 can help arrange open windows. Refer to Figure 19 as you complete Step 2.

FIGURE 19 Working with Two Windows ➤

a. Click the **Start button**. Click **Documents** in the right pane. Click the **Start button**. Click **Pictures** in the right pane.

> **TROUBLESHOOTING:** If the two windows open so that one is directly on top of the other, obscuring the lower window, click and drag the title bar of the topmost window to move the window so that you can see both.

You have opened two windows—Pictures and Documents. You are going to show students various ways to arrange the open windows. The two open windows are most likely overlapped, but if yours are not, that's OK. Just make sure both windows are open.

b. Right-click an empty part of the taskbar. Click **Show windows stacked**. Compare your desktop with Figure 19.

The contents of the windows will vary, but the arrangement should be similar.

> **TROUBLESHOOTING:** If your desktop displays more than two stacked windows, you have more than two windows open. You should make sure that only the Pictures and Documents windows are open. Close any others by right-clicking the corresponding taskbar icon and clicking Close window.

c. Right-click an empty part of the taskbar. Click **Show windows side by side**.

The two windows should line up vertically.

d. Click the **Close button** in both windows to close them.

e. Click the **Start button**. Click **Computer**. Click the **Start button**. Click **Control Panel**.

> **TROUBLESHOOTING:** If either window opens at full size (maximized), click the Restore Down button (middle button) at the top right side of the title bar to make the window smaller.

You have opened two windows—Computer and Control Panel. You will use the Windows Snap feature to position each window on a side of the desktop.

f. Click and drag the title bar of one of the windows to one side of the desktop. Keep dragging the window, even beyond the desktop edge, until a window outline appears. Release the mouse button. Do the same for the other window, snapping it to the opposite side of the desktop.

Both windows should be evenly spaced, each occupying half of the desktop.

g. Close both windows. (Click the **Close button** in the top right corner of each.)

STEP 3 ⟩ ADD AND REMOVE GADGETS, ADD SHORTCUTS TO THE DESKTOP, IDENTIFY ICONS

Not only do you want students to understand the basics of managing windows, but you know that they will also enjoy customizing the desktop. They need to know how to identify icons. They will also benefit from creating program shortcuts and adding gadgets for constantly changing items like the weather or a clock. Refer to Figure 20 as you complete Step 3.

FIGURE 20 Taskbar and Start Menu Properties ➤

a. Note any icons on the desktop that have an arrow in the bottom left corner. They represent programs or system resources. Double-click an icon to open the item window. Close the window by clicking the **Close button** in the top right corner.

b. Right-click an empty area of the taskbar. Click **Properties**. Click the **Auto-hide the taskbar check box** (unless a checkmark already appears), as shown in Figure 20. Click **OK**.

The taskbar will only show if you place the mouse pointer near where it should show. When you move the mouse pointer away, the taskbar disappears. You will explain to students that they can use the Taskbar and Start Menu Properties dialog box to customize the appearance and behavior of the taskbar.

c. Move the mouse pointer to the location of the taskbar. Right-click an empty area of the taskbar. Click **Properties**. Click to deselect the **Auto-hide the taskbar check box**. Click **OK**.

d. Click the **Start button**. Point to **All Programs**. Click **Accessories**. Right-click and drag Paint to the desktop. Release the mouse button. Click **Create shortcuts here**.

> **TROUBLESHOOTING:** To create a shortcut on the desktop, you must be able to see the desktop. Therefore, all windows should be closed before you click and drag the program from the Start menu. Also, be sure to use the right mouse button to click and drag, not the left.

You have placed a program shortcut on the desktop so that you can easily find it later. The arrow in the lower-left corner of the Paint icon indicates that it is a shortcut.

e. Right-click the **Paint shortcut icon** on the desktop. Click **Delete**. Click **Yes** to confirm the deletion.

Because you want to leave the classroom's computer just as you found it, you will delete the Paint shortcut from the desktop.

f. Right-click an empty area of the desktop. Click **Gadgets**. Double-click **Clock**. The Clock gadget appears on the right side of the desktop. Double-click **Weather** to add a Weather gadget.

> **TROUBLESHOOTING:** You must be connected to the Internet for the Weather gadget to display. If you are not connected, you will see a note to that effect where the gadget would have been placed.

g. Right-click the **Clock gadget** and click **Close gadget**. Do the same for the Weather gadget.

Because you want to leave the classroom's computer as you found it, you will close the Clock and Weather gadgets.

h. Click the **Close button** to close the Gadgets window.

STEP 4 ▶ EXPLORE THE START MENU, PIN ITEMS TO THE START MENU, CUSTOMIZE THE TASKBAR, PIN ITEMS TO THE TASKBAR

Upon completing the fifth grade, the students with whom you are working will advance to middle school. There, they will be expected to be comfortable with Windows 7. You will be with them for only a couple of class sessions, so you want to use your time to make sure they are introduced to the Start menu, understand the purpose of icons, and are confident with customizing the taskbar. With just a little practice, they will be well-prepared for middle school computer work. Refer to Figure 21 as you complete Step 4.

FIGURE 21 Pin a Program to Start Menu ➤

a. Click the **Start button**. Note the programs that display on the left side of the menu. Take a look at the right side of the menu. Click **Pictures**. Close the window that represents the Pictures folder.

You will explain to students that the left side of the Start menu contains commonly accessed programs or those that have been pinned to the Start menu. The right side includes system folders, such as Pictures, Documents, and Music; the Control Panel; and Help and Support. The Search box, located at the bottom left side of the Start menu, enables searches based on keywords.

b. Click the **Start button**. Point to **All Programs**. Click **Accessories**. Scroll, if necessary, to show Paint. Right-click **Paint**. Click **Pin to Start Menu**, as shown in Figure 21. Click outside the Start menu to remove it from view.

The example you will give students is that in some classes they will have a recurring need to open the Paint program. You want them to practice pinning the program to the Start menu.

c. Click the **Start button**. Check to make sure Paint appears on the left side of the menu. Click **Paint** to open it. Click the **Close button** to close the program.

> **TROUBLESHOOTING:** If you have recently opened Paint files, you might find it necessary to click Paint twice to open the program.

d. Click the **Start button**. Note that because Paint is a pinned program, it appears above the line on the left side of the Start menu. Right-click **Paint**. Click **Unpin from Start Menu**. Click outside the Start menu to remove it from view.

Because you want to leave the classroom's computer as you found it, you will unpin the Paint program from the Start menu.

e. Click the **Start button**. Point to **All Programs**. Click **Accessories**. Point to WordPad and right-click. Click **Pin to Taskbar**. Click outside the Start menu to remove the menu from view.

Students will need to know that if they open a program often, it is easy to pin it to the taskbar for quick access. That way, they won't have to find it on the Start menu or double-click an icon on the desktop. Instead, they can single-click the icon on the taskbar.

f. Click the **WordPad icon** on the taskbar. If you are not sure which icon is WordPad, place the mouse pointer over any icon and see the program name. Then locate WordPad. After WordPad opens, close it. Right-click the **WordPad icon** on the taskbar and click **Unpin this program from taskbar**.

After demonstrating the use of a pinned icon (by opening the associated program), you remove the pinned icon from the taskbar.

STEP 5 ▶ CHANGE THE DESKTOP BACKGROUND AND SCREEN SAVER

To end the class session on a creative note, you want the students to have fun changing the desktop background and experimenting with screen savers. Refer to Figures 22 and 23 as you complete Step 5.

> **TROUBLESHOOTING:** If you are working in a campus lab, you might not be able to change the desktop background or screen saver. In that case, you cannot complete this step of the Hands-On Exercise.

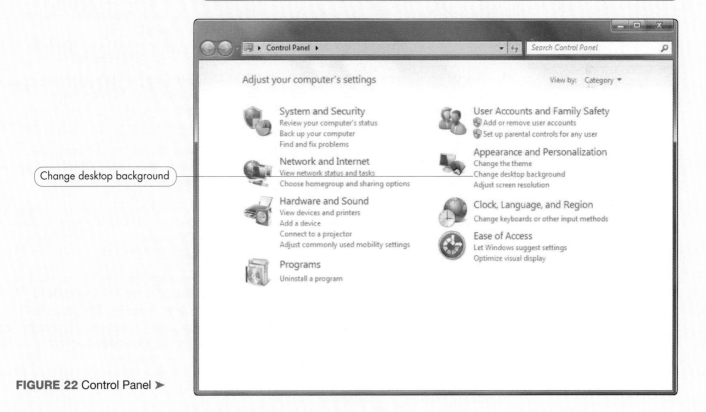

FIGURE 22 Control Panel ▶

Select picture location

Scroll bar

Select picture position

FIGURE 23 Selecting a background ➤

a. Click the **Start button**. Click **Control Panel**. As shown in Figure 22, click **Change desktop background** in the *Appearance and Personalization* section. Make sure **Windows Desktop Backgrounds** appears in the Picture location (see Figure 23). If not, click the **Picture location arrow**, and then select **Windows Desktop Backgrounds**.

b. Use the scroll bar to adjust the display of backgrounds and click to select one that you like. Check the *Picture position* area to make sure *Fill* is selected. If your instructor allows you to change the background, click **Save changes**. Otherwise, click **Cancel**.

c. Close any open windows to view the new desktop background if it was changed.

d. Click the **Start button**. Click **Control Panel**. Click **Change desktop background** (under Appearance and Personalization). Click **Browse**. Click **Libraries**. Click **Pictures**. Click **Public Pictures**. Click **Sample Pictures**. Click **OK**. Click a picture to select it as your background. Click the **Picture position button** and select **Center**.

It is fun to include a personal picture as a background. Here, you select a picture from the Sample Pictures folder (although you could just as easily select one of your pictures from a folder of your choice). You then center the picture on the background and will select a border color in the next step.

e. Click **Change background color**. Select a color from the palette. Click **OK**. If your instructor allows you to change the background, click **Save changes**. Otherwise, click **Cancel**. Close any open windows to view the new background if it was changed.

f. Click the **Start button**. Click **Control Panel**. Click **Appearance and Personalization**. Click **Change screen saver** (under *Personalization*). Click the **arrow** under *Screen saver*. Select a screen saver. Click **Preview**. Press **Esc** to remove the screen saver from view. Note that you can also change the Wait time to specify the number of minutes the computer must remain idle before the screen saver appears. Click **Cancel** to avoid making the change permanent, or **OK** if you are allowed to change the screen saver. Close any open windows.

Unless you saved the screen saver change and unless you wait the required wait time for the screen saver to appear, you will see no changes.

Windows Programs and Security Features

Windows 7 is a full-featured operating system, including built-in programs for such tasks as word processing, creating graphics, and system security. With only a little effort, you can learn to use those programs. Regardless of how many programs you install on your computer system, you can take comfort in knowing that you will always have access to software supporting basic tasks and that your computer is protected against spyware and hacking. In this section, you will learn to work with Windows 7 accessory and security programs.

> You can take comfort in knowing that you will always have access to software supporting basic tasks and that your computer is protected against spyware and hacking.

Identifying Windows Accessories

You use a computer for many purposes, but a primary reason to enjoy a computer is to run programs. A program is software that accomplishes a specific task. You use a word processing program to prepare documents, an e-mail program to compose and send e-mail, and a database program to maintain records. You can customize a computer by installing programs of your choice. Windows 7 provides a few programs for basic tasks, as well. Those programs include WordPad, Notepad, Paint, Snipping Tool, and Calculator.

Use Notepad and WordPad

Notepad is a text editing program built in to Windows 7.

WordPad is a basic word processing program built in to Windows 7.

Notepad and *WordPad* are programs that enable you to create and print documents. Notepad is a basic text editing program used primarily to edit text files, files that are identified with a .txt extension. Programmers sometimes use Notepad to prepare basic program statements. Notepad is not at all concerned with style and does not include the features of typical word processing software such as document formatting and character design.

WordPad, on the other hand, is a basic word processing program, and includes the capability of formatting text and inserting graphics. Not as full-featured as Microsoft Word, WordPad is still a handy alternative when you do not have access to Word or when you want to quickly create a simple document. WordPad saves documents in a Microsoft Word format, so you can open WordPad files in Word.

Figure 24 shows both WordPad and Notepad windows. Note the bare-bones appearance of Notepad when compared with WordPad. Access either program by clicking the Start button. Point to All Programs. Click Accessories. Make a program selection.

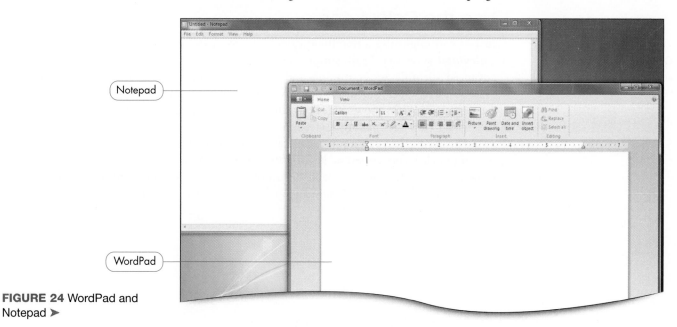

FIGURE 24 WordPad and Notepad ➤

Use Paint

Paint is a Windows 7 accessory that enables you to create graphics by drawing and adding text.

Paint is a Windows 7 program that enables you to create drawings and to open digital pictures. You will recall that you opened Paint in Hands-On Exercise 1. Figure 25 shows the Paint interface. Note the Ribbon at the top of the Paint window that includes such items as the Pencil tool, Brushes, Colors, and Shapes. Open Paint by clicking the Start button, All Programs, Accessories, and Paint. The palette in the center of the Paint window acts as an easel on which you can draw.

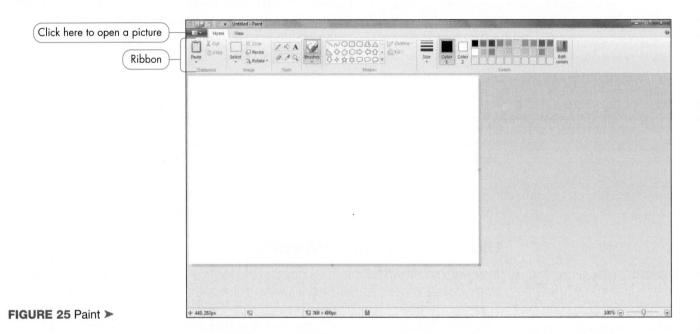

FIGURE 25 Paint ➤

When you open Paint, you can create and save a colorful drawing, including text, shapes, and background color. You can also open a digital photo and add comments, shapes, or drawings. If you want to work with an existing picture, open the photo by clicking the button in the top left corner of the Paint window (see Figure 25). Click Open, browse to the location of the picture, and double-click the picture. Then use Paint tools to add to the picture, saving it when done.

Use the Calculator

Calculator is a Windows 7 accessory that acts as a handheld calculator with different views—standard, scientific, programming, and statistical.

Just as you might use a handheld calculator, you can take advantage of the Windows 7 *Calculator* accessory. From simple addition, subtraction, multiplication, and division to advanced scientific, programming, and statistical functions, Calculator is a very handy tool to be aware of. Open Calculator by clicking the Start button, All Programs, Accessories, and Calculator. Figure 26 shows all four Calculator versions. Change from one version to another by clicking View and making a selection.

When using Calculator, you can either type numeric entries and operators $(+, -, *, \text{and} /)$ or you can click corresponding keys on the calculator. You can also use the numeric keypad, usually found to the right of the keyboard on a desktop computer. Laptops do not typically have a numeric keypad but often include a function key that you can press to use alternate keys as a numeric keypad.

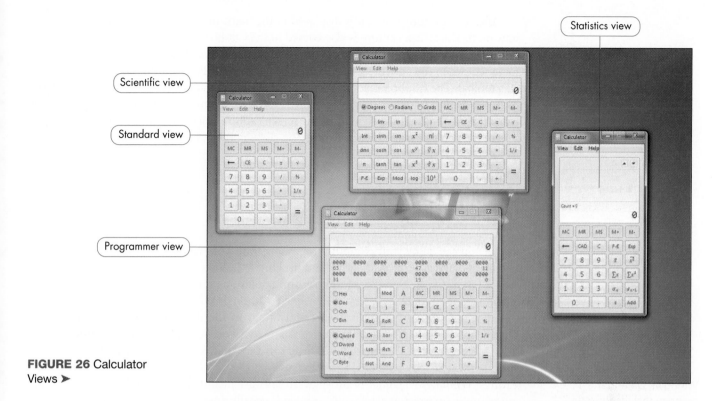

Scientific view

Standard view

Programmer view

FIGURE 26 Calculator Views ➤

TIP Use Sticky Notes

Sticky Notes is a fun and useful Windows 7 accessory. Open Sticky Notes by clicking the Start button, All Programs, Accessories, and Sticky Notes. Use the program as you would a paper sticky note, recording to-do lists, phone numbers, or anything else. Your notes appear as stick-up notes on the desktop. Click the New Note button to add another note, click the Delete Note button to delete a note, and right-click a note to change the color.

Use the Snipping Tool

The **Snipping Tool** is a Windows 7 accessory that enables you to capture and save a screen display.

A **snip** is a screen display that you have captured with the Snipping Tool.

The *Snipping Tool* is a Windows 7 accessory program that enables you to capture, or *snip*, a screen display so that you can save, annotate, or share it. On occasion, you might need to capture an image of the screen for use in a report or to document an error for later troubleshooting. Using the Snipping Tool (see Figure 27), you can capture screen elements in a rectangular, free-form, window, or full-screen fashion. Then you can draw on or annotate the screen captures, save them, or send them to others.

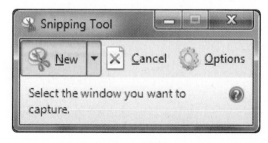

FIGURE 27 Snipping Tool ➤

Open the Snipping Tool by clicking the Start button, All Programs, Accessories, and Snipping Tool. Click the arrow next to the New button and select a snip type (rectangular, free-form, etc.). If you select a window snip type, you will click the window to capture. If you select rectangular or free-form, you must click and drag to identify the area to capture. Of course, it is not necessary to specify an area when you select full-screen capture.

After you capture a snip, it is displayed in the mark-up window, where you can write or draw on it. The screen capture is also copied to the Clipboard, which is a temporary holding area in your computer's memory. You can then paste the screen capture in a word processing document when the document is displayed by clicking the Paste button on the word processor's toolbar. The Clipboard is temporary storage only. Because the Clipboard's contents are lost when your computer is powered down, you should immediately paste a copied screen image if it is your intention to include the screen capture in a document or other application. Otherwise, you can save a screen capture by clicking the Save Snip button and indicating a location and file name for the snip.

Working with Security Settings and Software

So that you can enjoy your computer for a long time, you will want to protect it from security threats such as viruses, spyware, and hacking. Windows 7 monitors your security status, providing recommendations for security settings and software updates as needed. Although Windows 7 provides a firewall and antispyware software, you should make sure your computer is also protected against viruses. Such protection requires that you install antivirus software that is not included with Windows 7.

Windows 7 monitors your security status, providing recommendations for security settings and software updates as needed.

Although you are not protected against viruses automatically, Windows 7 does have security features. *Windows Defender* is antispyware software included with Windows 7. It identifies and removes *spyware*, which is software that is usually downloaded without your awareness, collecting personal information from your computer. Windows 7 also includes a *firewall* to protect against unauthorized access (hacking).

Windows Defender is a program that identifies and removes spyware.

Spyware is software that gathers information through a user's Internet connection, usually for advertising purposes. Spyware is most often installed without a user's permission.

A **firewall** is software or hardware that protects a computer or network from unauthorized access.

Understand the Action Center

Windows 7 monitors your system for various maintenance and security settings, recommending action through the Action Center when necessary. Open the Action Center by clicking the Start button, Control Panel, System and Security, and then Action Center. In

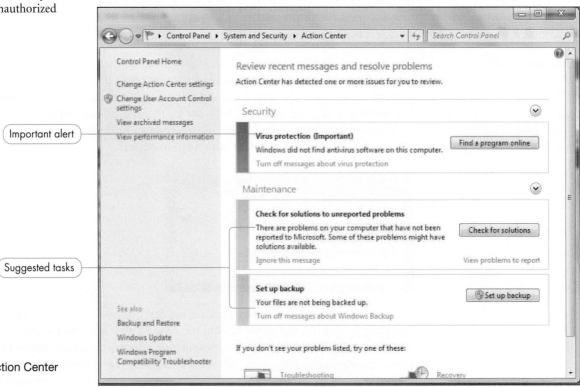

FIGURE 28 Action Center Alerts ➤

Figure 28, the Action Center gives several messages in order of severity. Red flags are for potentially serious or important alerts that should be addressed soon. Yellow items are suggested tasks, usually maintenance such as backing up files. For a quick summary of Action Center items, you can click the Action Center icon in the Notification area. Click a link on the summary list to explore a recommended action. When the status of a monitored item changes, perhaps when antivirus software becomes out of date, Action Center will display a message in a balloon (pop-up) on the Notification area (see Figure 29).

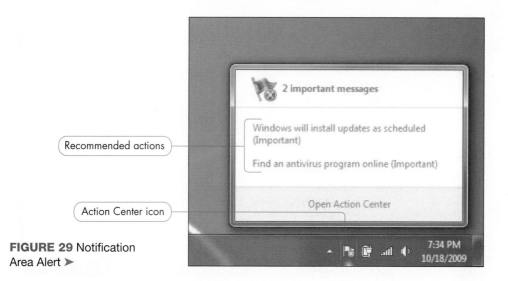

FIGURE 29 Notification Area Alert ➤

Use Windows Defender

You probably enjoy accessing Web sites and downloading programs. Although such activity is a great way to have fun, it carries a serious risk—downloading spyware along with the program. Actually, spyware can be installed on your computer whenever you connect to the Internet, regardless of whether you download anything. Spyware is usually installed without your knowledge. It can do anything from keeping track of Web sites you visit (for marketing purposes) to changing browser settings to recording keystrokes. Obviously, spyware is unwelcome and a potential security risk.

Windows Defender is antispyware software that is included with Windows 7. Windows Defender can be set to run in real time, which means that it is always on guard against spyware, alerting you when spyware attempts to install itself or change your computer settings. You can also schedule routine scans so that Windows Defender checks your system for malicious software. Open Windows Defender by clicking the Start button, typing Windows Defender in the Search box, and pressing Enter (or clicking the corresponding link in the Results list). Figure 30 shows the Windows Defender program window.

Customize User Account Control

User Account Control (UAC) is a Windows feature that asks for your permission before allowing any changes to your computer settings.

User Account Control (UAC) is a Windows feature that asks for your permission before allowing a program to make a change to your system settings. Although such information is sometimes helpful, you might prefer to be notified only when substantial changes are attempted; that way, you are not interrupted quite as often. Windows Vista, the previous version of Windows, was noted for what some users considered excessive UAC prompts.

If you have only one user account on your computer, it is an administrator-level account. Most likely, you are the administrator, which means that only you can respond to UAC messages. Other user accounts are considered standard accounts, with varying levels of permissions that you can choose to grant.

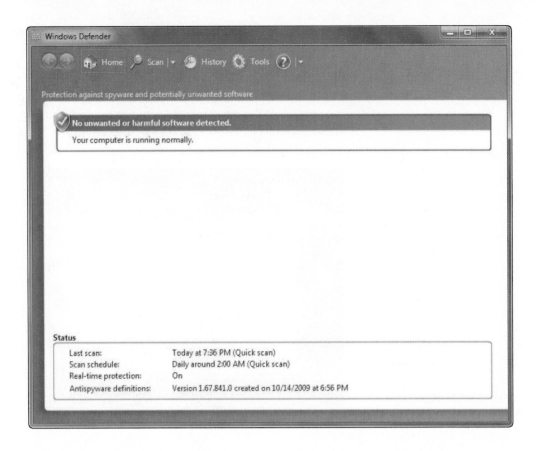

FIGURE 30 Windows
Defender ➤

You might want to be informed of any changes that occur, even those that you initiate, that change your Windows settings. Or perhaps you prefer to know of only those changes attempted by programs. In either case, you can modify the level of UAC through the Action Center. Click the Start button, Control Panel, System and Security, and then Action Center. Click Change User Account Control settings. Adjust the bar in the dialog box shown in Figure 31.

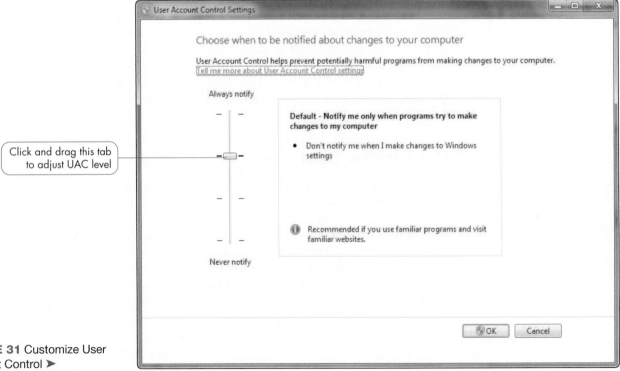

Click and drag this tab
to adjust UAC level

FIGURE 31 Customize User
Account Control ➤

Access Windows Update

As you are probably well aware, there is no perfect product. Windows 7 is no exception. Even long after the operating system is produced, Microsoft will undoubtedly identify ways to enhance its security or fix problems that occur. There is no need to download or purchase an updated operating system each time changes are necessary; instead, you can simply make sure that your computer is set to automatically download any updates (fixes). Such modifications to the operating system are called ***Windows Updates.***

Windows Updates are additions to the operating system that prevent or correct problems, including security concerns.

Microsoft strongly recommends that you configure your computer to automatically download and install any updates. That way, you do not have to remember to check for updates or manually download them. To schedule automatic updates, click the Start button, All Programs, and then Windows Update. Click Change settings. As shown in Figure 32, you can click to select the level of updates. You can have Windows both download and install updates automatically (strongly recommended), only download but let you install them, or never check for updates (certainly not recommended!). You can also schedule a time for updates to occur.

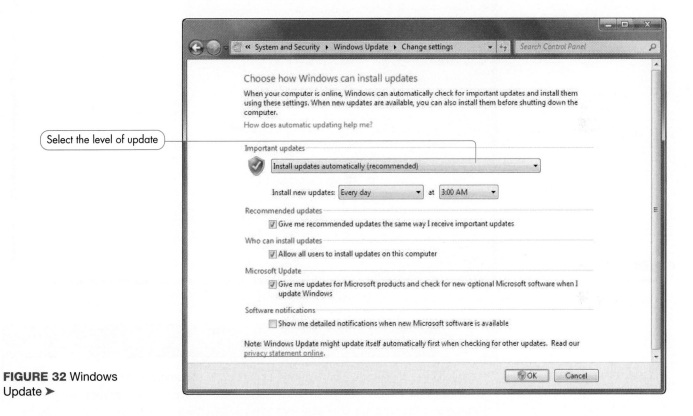

FIGURE 32 Windows Update ➤

Even between scheduled downloads, you can have your computer check for updates. Click the Start button, All Programs, Windows Update, and then Check for updates. If you want to check for updates for other Microsoft products, such as Microsoft Office, open Windows Update, and click Change settings. Select Give me updates for Microsoft products and check for new optional Microsoft software when I update Windows.

Use Windows Firewall

When you work with the Internet, there is always a possibility that a self-replicating virus or another user could disable your computer or view its contents. To keep that from occurring, it is imperative that you use firewall software. Windows 7 includes firewall software that is active when the operating system is installed. It remains on guard whenever your computer is on, protecting against both unauthorized incoming traffic and outgoing. That means that other people, computers, or programs are not allowed to communicate with your computer unless you give permission. Also, programs on your system are not allowed to communicate online unless you approve them.

Periodically, you might want to check to make sure your firewall has not been turned off accidentally. Click the Start button, Control Panel, System and Security, and then Check firewall status (under Windows Firewall). From the dialog box (see Figure 33), you can turn the firewall on or off. You can also adjust other firewall settings.

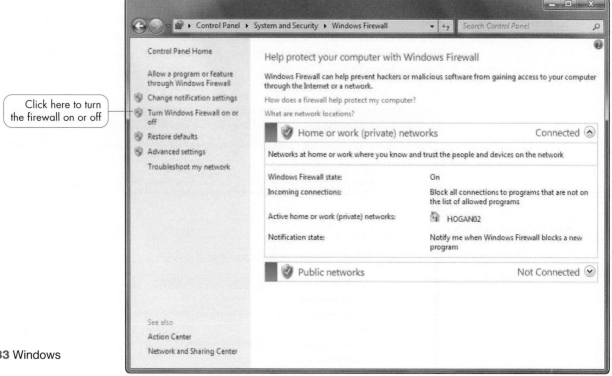

Click here to turn the firewall on or off

FIGURE 33 Windows Firewall ➤

> ## TIP Set Up Parental Controls
>
> If children in your household have user accounts on your computer, you can set up parental controls to limit the hours they can use the computer, the types of games they can play, and the programs they can run. User accounts that you limit must be standard accounts. You cannot apply parental controls to a guest account, which is an account type reserved for people who use your computer on a temporary basis. If you plan to use parental controls, it is a good idea to turn off the guest account (open the Control Panel, click Add or remove user accounts, click Guest, click Turn off the guest account). Open the Control Panel to create user accounts and assign standard privileges. To assign parental controls, open the Control Panel and click Set up parental controls for any user (under User Accounts and Family Safety). After selecting the user account to limit, apply any parental controls.

Getting Started with Windows 7

HANDS-ON EXERCISES

2 Windows Programs and Security Features

Windows is a gateway to using application software. You know that the fifth-grade students are most interested in the "fun" things that can be done with software. You want to excite them about having fun with a computer but you also want them to understand that along with the fun comes some concern about security and privacy. In this section of your demonstration, you will encourage them to explore software and to understand how Windows can help address security concerns.

Skills covered: Create a WordPad Document, Use Calculator • Use the Action Center to Check Security and Privacy Settings • Use the Snipping Tool.

STEP 1 ▶ CREATE A WORDPAD DOCUMENT, USE CALCULATOR

Because all computers are configured with different software, your demonstration to the class will focus on only those programs (software) that are built in to Windows (those that students are most likely to find on any computer). Specifically, you will use WordPad and Calculator for your brief discussion. Refer to Figure 34 as you complete Step 1.

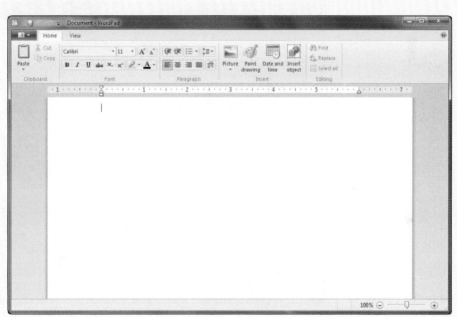

FIGURE 34 WordPad ▶

a. Click the **Start button**. Point to **All Programs**. Click **Accessories**. Click **WordPad**. The WordPad window opens, as shown in Figure 34.

WordPad is a word processing program that is installed along with Windows 7 (and earlier Windows versions).

b. Be sure the insertion point is located in the WordPad window. Type your **first and last names**. Press **Enter**. Type your **street address**. Press **Enter**. Type your **city**, **state**, and **zip**.

> **TROUBLESHOOTING:** Before typing your name, you should see a blinking black bar (insertion point) in the white WordPad document area. If you do not, click in the document area to position the insertion point.

c. Close the WordPad document. Click **Don't Save** when prompted to save your changes.

Having demonstrated the use of a word processor, you will close the document without saving it.

d. Click the **Start button**. Point to **All Programs**. Click **Accessories**. Click **Calculator**. Click **View**. If you do not see a bullet beside *Standard*, click **Standard**. If you do see a bullet beside *Standard*, press **Esc** (on the keyboard).

e. Click the corresponding keys on the calculator to complete the following formula: **87+98+100/3**. Click the = sign when you have typed the formula.

You use the calculator to show how a student might determine his average, assuming he has taken three exams (weighted equally) with scores of 87, 98, and 100. The result should be 95.

f. Close the Calculator.

STEP 2 ▶ USE THE ACTION CENTER TO CHECK SECURITY AND PRIVACY SETTINGS

The Action Center will occasionally display messages regarding security and privacy settings. You want the Cedar Cove students to be aware of how important those messages are, so you will show them how to use the Action Center. Refer to Figure 35 as you complete Step 2.

> **TROUBLESHOOTING:** If you are working in a campus lab, you might not have access to the Action Center or Windows Update. In that case, you should proceed to Step 3 of this Hands-On Exercise.

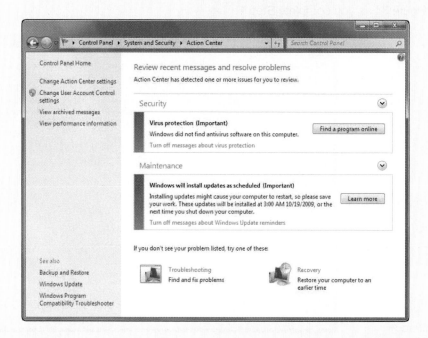

FIGURE 35 Action Center ➤

a. Click the **Start button**. Click **Control Panel**. Click **System and Security**. Click **Action Center**.

Although any alerts displayed on your computer may vary from those shown in Figure 35, the general appearance should be similar.

b. Click **Change Action Center settings**. Take a look at the items monitored by the Action Center. Note that you can select or deselect any of them. Click **Cancel**. Close the Action Center.

c. Click the **Start button**. Point to **All Programs**. Scroll through the list of programs if necessary and click **Windows Update**. Click **Change settings**. Is your system scheduled for a routine check for or installation of updates? Click the **Back button** (arrow pointing left at the top left corner of the window).

d. Click **View update history**. You should see a summary of recent updates and their level of importance. Click **OK**. Close any open windows.

As students progress and are required to use a computer in many facets of their education, they might find occasion to include screen captures in reports or presentations. Windows 7 includes a Snipping Tool that enables you to select any part of the screen and save it as a picture file. You plan to present the Snipping Tool to the Cedar Cove class. Refer to Figures 36 and 37 as you complete Step 3.

FIGURE 36 Snipping Tool ➤

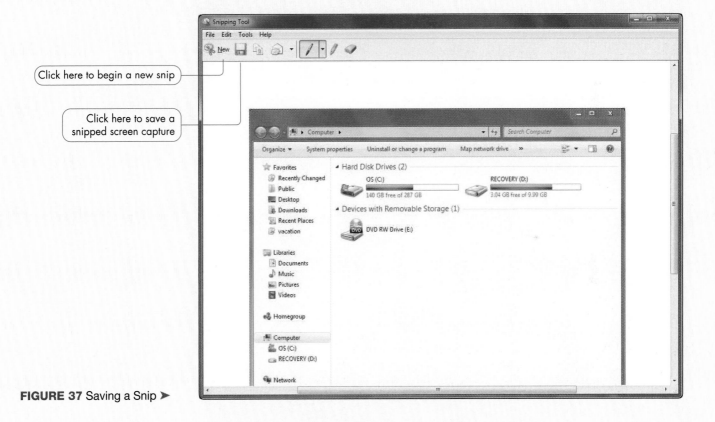

FIGURE 37 Saving a Snip ➤

a. Click the **Start button**. Click **Computer**. If the Computer window opens in full size (maximized), click the **Restore Down button** to reduce the window size.

Assume that as part of a report, students are to insert a picture of the Computer window. Perhaps the report is on computer concepts and the student wants to include the Computer window as an illustration of a computer configuration. After opening the Computer window, you will illustrate the use of the Snipping Tool to capture the screen in a picture file.

b. Click the **Start button**. Point to **All Programs**. Click **Accessories**. Click **Snipping Tool**. The Snipping Tool displays as shown in Figure 36. Click the **New arrow**. Click **Window Snip**. Click in the Computer window to select it.

You have selected a window as a screen capture.

c. Click the **Save Snip** icon in the Snipping Tool window (see Figure 37). Scroll up in the left pane of the Save As dialog box if necessary and click **Favorites**. Click **Desktop (in the left pane, not the right)**. Click in the **File name box** (where you most likely see the word *Capture*). Click and drag to select the word *Capture* (if it is not already selected). Type **Computer window** (to change the file name). Click **Save**.

You have saved the picture of the Computer window to the desktop.

d. Close any open windows. You should see the *Computer window* file on the desktop. Double-click to open it. Close the file.

e. Right-click **Computer window** on the desktop. Click **Delete**. Confirm the deletion.

You will remove the file from the desktop.

Windows Search and Help

No matter how well prepared you are or how much you know about your computer, you will occasionally have questions about a process or tool. And no matter how careful you are to save files in locations that will be easily located later, you will sometimes lose track of a file or folder. In those cases, Windows 7 can help! You can take advantage of an extensive Help and Support library to get some questions answered and you can search for items, using anything that you know—part of the file name, the file type, or even a bit of the contents. In this section, you will learn to search for items such as files, folders, and programs. You will also explore the Help and Support feature.

> You can take advantage of an extensive Help and Support library to get some questions answered and you can search for items, using anything that you know.

Performing a Search

If you know anything about an item you are looking for, you are likely to find it if it is on your computer. Windows 7 provides several ways to search. You can use the Search box found on the Start menu or you can use the Search box located at the top right corner of some open windows. You can customize a search to look at specific folders, libraries, or storage media, and you can narrow the search by filters (file type, date modified, etc.). After conducting a search, you can save it so that you can access it later without re-creating search criteria.

Conduct a Search

> A **tag** is a custom file property that you create to further identify a file. A tag could be a rating that you apply to a file. You can set tags and view file properties in the details pane of a window.

> A **file property** is an identifier of a file, such as author or date created. You can find file properties in the details pane of a window.

You will find a Search box on the Start menu and at the top right corner of most open windows (see Figure 38). You will probably find the Search box on the Start menu the most convenient place to begin a search. You can find files, folders, programs, and e-mail messages saved on your computer by entering one or more keywords in the Search box. As you type, items that match your search will appear in the list above the Search box. Click any item to be directed to that location or file. The search will occur based on text in the file, text in the file name, *tags*, and other *file properties*.

> You can find files, folders, programs, and e-mail messages saved on your computer by entering one or more keywords in the Search box.

FIGURE 38 Search Box on the Start Menu and in a Window ➤

If you are certain a program is installed on your computer, but you cannot find the program on the Start menu or elsewhere, or perhaps you just don't know where to find the program, you can type some or all of the program name in the Search box on the Start menu. Immediately, you will see any matching program names in the list above. Simply click the name in the list to open the program.

When you perform a search, Windows 7 searches quickly through indexed locations. All folders in Libraries are automatically included in an index. If you search in locations that are not indexed, the search can be much slower than it would be otherwise. To get a list of indexed locations and to add additional folders or disk drives to the index, click the Start button and type Indexing Options in the Search box. Click Indexing Options from the list that displays above. If you want to add locations, click Modify.

Suppose you cannot find a document that you feel sure you saved in the Documents folder. Open the Documents folder (click the Start button and click Documents). Click in the Search box at the top right corner of the Documents window. Type any identifier (part or all of the file name, some file contents, or a file tag or property). As you type, any matching file in the Documents folder is displayed.

When you conduct a search through a window (not the Start menu), only the contents of the current folder are searched. You can expand the search to include other folders or libraries and other storage media. You can also narrow the search to seek only specific file types or for properties specific to the folder. For example, if you are searching for music in the Music folder, you might want to narrow the search to a particular artist.

Expand or Narrow a Search

To expand the search, begin typing a search term in the Search box of a window and then scroll to the bottom of the list of search results. Point to a selection in the Search again in area (see Figure 39) and select another area to search. Selecting Computer searches the entire computer system, even those areas that are not indexed, as well as Libraries (including Documents, Music, Pictures, and Videos). Use Custom to search a specific location, or Internet to search online.

To narrow a search, click in the Search box of a window and click the appropriate search filter below the search area. Depending on the folder or file type you are searching for, specific filters will vary. Figure 40 shows a search of the Pictures folder for any files containing

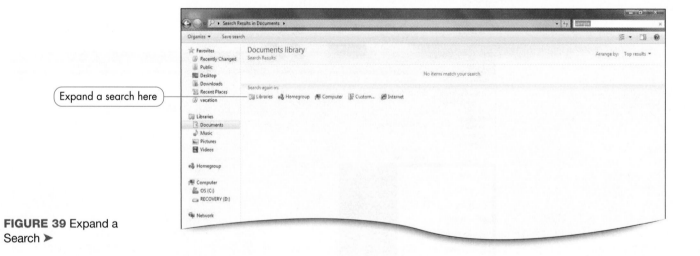

Expand a search here

FIGURE 39 Expand a Search ➤

the word *Vacation*. The search will be narrowed by selecting the Date Taken filter. Simply click an option to filter by and indicate the criteria. The way you enter criteria depends on the filter selected. For example, you might simply click to select an artist in the Music folder, whereas you could indicate a range of dates to narrow a search of Pictures.

FIGURE 40 Narrow a
Search ➤

Save a Search

If you know that you will conduct the same search often, you might find it helpful to save the search so that you do not have to continually enter the same search criteria. Perform the search once. On the toolbar, click Save search. Type a name for the search and click Save. The next time you want to conduct the search, open the Computer window. The saved search name is displayed in the Favorites section, as shown in Figure 41. Simply click the link to get new results.

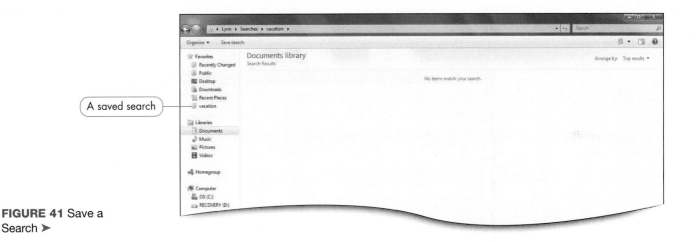

FIGURE 41 Save a
Search ➤

Getting Help

Help and Support is available from the Start menu, providing assistance with specific questions or providing broad discussions of Windows features.

Help on almost any Windows topic is only a click away using ***Help and Support***. As you find that you need assistance on a topic or procedure, click the Start button and click Help and Support. You can then browse the help library by topic or search the library by typing keywords. Use the Remote Assistance feature (accessible after you click More support options in the lower-left corner of the Windows Help and Support window) if you want to ask someone to help with a computer problem from a distance. You can even take advantage of Microsoft's extensive online help. Help is also available within a dialog box and within a software application. Obviously, help can be found wherever you need it!

Help on almost any Windows topic is only a click away using Help and Support.

Search and Browse Help

Most often, you know exactly what you need assistance with. In that case, click in the Search box of Help and Support (see Figure 42), and type your topic. For example, if you are seeking information on resizing desktop icons, type *resize desktop icons.* Press Enter. A list of results displays, arranged in order of usefulness. Click any topic to view more detail. You can print results by clicking the Print button.

FIGURE 42 Help and Support ➤

Help topics are also available when you browse help by clicking the Browse Help button (see Figure 42). By browsing the subsequent list of topics, you can learn a lot about Windows. You might browse Help and Support when you have no particular need for topic-specific assistance or when your question is very general. Figure 43 summarizes topics that you can select from when you browse Help.

FIGURE 43 Browse Topics ➤

Windows Help and Support is an excellent tool when you need assistance on general topics related to the operating system, but you might also need help with a specific application, as well. For example, you will be working with a software application, such as a word processing program, and find that you have a question. Invariably, you can locate a Help button that enables you to type search terms or browse application-specific help topics. When you are working with a task in an application, you will often be responding to a dialog box. If you have a question at that time, click the ? button, usually located in the top right corner of a window, for help related to the specific task. Some dialog boxes, but not all, include a Help button. Figure 44 shows a dialog box with a Help button.

Help button

FIGURE 44 Dialog Box Help ➤

Get Remote Assistance

Undoubtedly, you will have trouble with your computer at some time and need some assistance. You might consider getting someone to help you by letting them connect to your computer remotely to determine the problem. Of course, you will only want to ask someone that you trust because that person will temporarily have access to your files.

Remote Assistance is available through Windows 7 Help and Support. Click the Start button, and then Help and Support. Click More support options, in the lower-left corner of the Windows Help and Support window. Click Windows Remote Assistance. Click an option to either invite someone you trust to help you or to help someone who has invited you. If the person who is helping you is also using Windows 7, you can use a method called Easy Connect. The first time you use Easy Connect to request assistance, you will receive a password that you then give to the person offering assistance. Using that password, the helper can remotely connect to your computer and exchange information. Thereafter, a password is not necessary—you simply click the contact information for the helper to initiate a session. If the person providing assistance is using another Windows operating system, you can use an invitation file, which is a file that you create that is sent (usually by e-mail) to the person offering assistance. The invitation file includes a password that is used to connect the two computers.

Get Online Help

So that you are sure to get the latest help, you will probably want to include online Help files in your searches for assistance. To make sure that is happening, open Help and Support, click Options, and then click Settings. Click to select Improve my search results by using online Help (recommended). Click OK. Of course, you must be connected to the Internet before accessing online Help.

HANDS-ON EXERCISES

3 Windows Search and Help

As you close your presentation to the Cedar Cove class, you want the students to be confident in their ability but well aware that help is available. You plan to demonstrate several ways they can get assistance. You also want them to know how to conduct searches for files and folders. Although they might not give it much thought, you know that there will be many times when they will forget where they saved a very important file. Therefore, it is imperative that you include the topic of searching in your presentation.

Skills covered: Explore Windows Help, Search Using Keywords • Use the Search Box to Conduct a Search, Expand a Search • Get Help in an Application, Get Help in a Dialog Box.

STEP 1 ▶ EXPLORE WINDOWS HELP, SEARCH USING KEYWORDS

As students in your class progress to middle and high school, they may have opportunities to use laptops for class work. They also are likely to find themselves in locations where they can connect to the Internet wirelessly. Using that example, you will help the class understand how to use Windows Help and Support to learn how to find and safely connect to an available wireless network. Refer to Figure 45 as you complete Step 1.

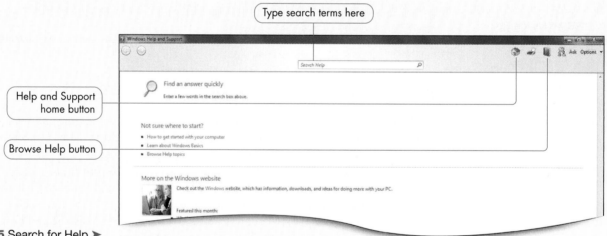

FIGURE 45 Search for Help ➤

a. Click the **Start button**. Click **Help and Support** in the right pane. Maximize the Windows Help and Support window.

> **TROUBLESHOOTING:** Your computer should be connected to the Internet before completing this exercise. That way, you can include online help resources.

b. Click the **Browse Help button**. Click **Networking—connecting computers and devices**. Click **Connecting to a network**. Click **View and connect to available wireless networks**. Read through the topic. Pay close attention to any warning about safely connecting to a wireless network.

You will show students how to use Help and Support browsing to locate help on a topic—in this case, connecting to a wireless network.

c. Click the **Help and Support home button**. Click in the **Search Help box** and type **Connect to a wireless network**. Press **Enter**. Click **View and connect to available wireless networks**.

Note that you arrived at the same topic as in the previous step, but took a different route. Close the Windows Help and Support window.

d. Use any method of getting Help and Support to answer the question "How can I make sure a wireless connection is secure?" What did you find?

STEP 2 ▶ **USE THE SEARCH BOX TO CONDUCT A SEARCH, EXPAND A SEARCH**

You want to show students how to search for files, but you are not familiar enough with the classroom computer to know what files to search for. You know, however, that Windows-based computers will include some picture files so you feel certain you can use the example of searching for files with a .jpg (picture) type. You will also illustrate expanding and narrowing a search. Refer to Figure 46 as you complete Step 2.

FIGURE 46 Narrow a Search ▶

a. Click the **Start button**. Click **Pictures**. Maximize the window. Click in the **Search Pictures box** and type **Tulips**. Double-click the *Tulips* file to open it. Close any open windows.

> **TROUBLESHOOTING:** If you do not find a Tulips file, place the student file CD in the CD drive. Wait a few seconds and close any dialog box that opens. In the Search again area, click Custom. Click the arrow beside Computer. Click the CD drive containing your student CD. Click OK. Navigate to the student data file for this chapter and double-click Tulips.

You search for a file by name—Tulips. Because one of the desktop backgrounds provided by Windows 7 is a file named Tulips, you should be able to find it on the classroom computer in the Pictures folder.

b. Click the **Start button**. Click **Pictures**. Maximize the window, if necessary. Click in the **Search Pictures box**. Look beneath the *Search* box to find the *Add a search filter* area. Click **Type**, as shown in Figure 46. Click **.jpg**. All files of that type should display to the left. Double-click any file to open it. Close the picture.

You want to find a few picture files that are saved in the Pictures folder. Because you know that many picture files are of the .jpg file type, you can limit the search to that file type.

c. Click Documents in the left pane. Click in the **Search Documents box** and type **Sample**. Regardless of whether any results are found, expand the search to include Libraries. Click **Libraries** in the *Search again in* area. Double-click the **Sample Music folder** to view the folder contents. Close all open windows.

d. Click the **Start button**. Click in the **Search box** on the Start menu, and type **Getting Started**. If more than one Getting Started link appears, place the mouse pointer over each link. Click the one with a ScreenTip that reads *Learn about Windows features and start* *using them.* Click **Go online to learn more**. You will be directed to a Microsoft Web page that provides information on Windows 7. Take a look, click any links that look interesting, and then close any open windows.

> **TROUBLESHOOTING:** After clicking Go online to learn more, you will view a Web page only if your computer is currently connected to the Internet.

Windows 7 provides a Getting Started tip box, but since you are not sure where that information resides, you will use the Search box on the Start menu to find it.

STEP 3 ▶ **GET HELP IN AN APPLICATION, GET HELP IN A DIALOG BOX**

As you complete the session with the fifth-graders, you want them to understand that they will never be without assistance. If they need help with general computer and operating system questions, they can access Help and Support from the Start menu. If they are working with an application, such as a word processor, they will most likely find a Help link that will enable them to search for help related to keywords. Within an application, if they have a dialog box open, they can sometimes get help related to the dialog box's activities. You will demonstrate application help and dialog box help. Refer to Figure 47 as you complete Step 3.

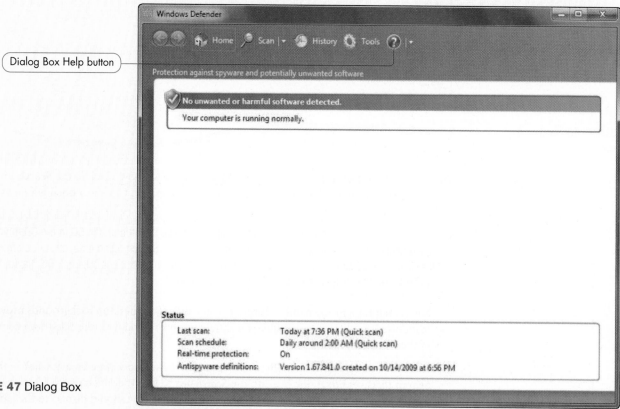

FIGURE 47 Dialog Box Help ▶

a. Click the **Start button**. Click in the **Search box** on the Start menu. Type **Windows Defender**. Click the **Windows Defender link** that appears in the results list.

b. Click the question mark (**?**) shown in Figure 47 on the right side of the Windows Defender toolbar. Maximize the Windows Help and Support window. Click **Scan for spyware and other potentially unwanted software**. Read about how to conduct a Windows Defender scan. Close all open windows.

c. Click the **Start button**. Click **Control Panel**. Click **Appearance and Personalization**. Click **Change the theme** in the *Personalization* section. Click the **?** in the top right corner of the dialog box to open dialog box Help. Read about themes. Close any open windows.

After reading this chapter, you have accomplished the following objectives.

1. Understand the desktop. The desktop is the display that appears when you turn on a computer. It contains icons (small pictures) that represent programs, files, folders, and system resources. The taskbar is the horizontal bar along the bottom of the desktop. It includes a Start button, pinned icons, icons of open windows, and the Notification area. You can customize the desktop to include a background and a screen saver.

2. Manage windows. Programs, folders, and other computer projects open in individual windows on the desktop, much like papers on a desk. You can manage windows by moving, resizing, stacking, or snapping them into position so that multiple windows are easier to work with and identify.

3. Identify Windows accessories. Windows 7 provides several accessory programs, including a word processor (WordPad), text editor (Notepad), calculator (Calculator), and screen capture tool (Snipping Tool). You will find accessory programs when you click the Start button, All Programs, and Accessories.

4. Work with security settings and software. Windows 7 takes computer security seriously, providing monitoring and software that helps keep your computer safe from spyware and hackers. Windows Defender, an antispyware program, is included with Windows and works to identify and remove instances of spyware. Spyware is unsolicited and unwelcome software that is often installed on your computer without your knowledge or permission. It can then track your Internet travel and modify your computer settings. The Action Center monitors the status of your security and maintenance settings, alerting you when maintenance tasks (such as backing up your system) are overlooked or when your security is at risk (when antivirus software is out of date, for example). A Windows firewall protects against unauthorized access to your computer from outside entities and prohibits Internet travel by programs from your computer without your permission.

5. Perform a search. As you work with a computer, it is inevitable that you will forget where you saved a file or that you misplace a file or folder. Windows 7 provides ample support for finding such items, providing a Search box on the Start menu and in every open window. As you type search keywords in either of those areas, Windows immediately begins a search, showing results. From an open window, you can begin a search and then narrow it by file type or other criteria unique to the searched folder. You might, for example, narrow a search by Date Taken if you are searching in the Pictures folder. You can also expand a search to include more search areas than the current folder.

6. Get Help. You can learn a lot about Windows by accessing the Help and Support features available with Windows 7. Get help when you click the Start button and Help and Support. If you are looking for specific answers, you can type search keyword(s) in the Search box and then click any resulting links. If your question is more general, you can browse Help by clicking the Browse Help button and then working through various links, learning as you go. Help is also available within an application by clicking a Help button and phrasing a search. If you are working with a dialog box, you can click a ? button for specific assistance with the task at hand.

KEY TERMS

Action Center	Notepad	Start menu
Aero Flip 3D	Notification area	Tag
Aero Peek	Operating system	Taskbar
Calculator	Paint	Title bar
Desktop	Pin	Toolbar
Dialog box	Screen saver	User Account Control (UAC)
File property	Shortcut	Window
Firewall	Snap	Windows Defender
Gadget	Snip	Windows Updates
Help and Support	Snipping Tool	WordPad
Icon	Spyware	
Jump List	Start button	

1. The Windows 7 feature that alerts you to any maintenance or security concerns is the:

    (a) Action Center

    (b) Security Center

    (c) Windows Defender

    (d) Control Panel

2. Snapping windows means that you:

    (a) Minimize all open windows simultaneously so that the desktop displays

    (b) Auto arrange all open windows so that they are of uniform size

    (c) Manually reposition all open windows so that you can see the content of each

    (d) Move any open windows to an opposing side of the desktop until they snap into place

3. Which of the following accessory programs is primarily a text editor?

    (a) Notepad

    (b) Snipping Tool

    (c) Journal

    (d) Calculator

4. A calendar, which is an example of a constantly changing desktop item, is a(n):

    (a) Icon

    (b) Thumbnail

    (c) Gadget

    (d) Action

5. Open windows are displayed as icons on the:

    (a) Desktop

    (b) Taskbar

    (c) Notification area

    (d) Start menu

6. A shortcut icon on the desktop is identified by:

    (a) An arrow at the lower-left corner of the icon

    (b) The word *shortcut* included as part of the icon name

    (c) A checkmark at the lower-left corner of the icon

    (d) Its placement on the right side of the desktop

7. Help and Support is available from which of the following?

    (a) Start menu

    (b) Desktop icon

    (c) Notification area

    (d) Taskbar

8. Which of the following is NOT a method of switching between open windows?

    (a) Alt+Tab

    (b) Shift+Tab

    (c) Click an open window icon on the taskbar

    (d) Windows logo+Tab

9. When you maximize a window, you:

    (a) Fill the screen with the window

    (b) Prioritize the window so that it is always placed on top of all other open windows

    (c) Expand the window's height but leave its width unchanged

    (d) Expand the window's width but leave its height unchanged

10. When you enter search keywords in the Search box of a folder window (such as the Documents window):

    (a) The search is not limited to the selected folder

    (b) The search cannot be further narrowed

    (c) The search is automatically expanded to include every folder on the hard drive

    (d) The search is limited to the selected folder, but can be expanded if you like

1 Senior Academy

As a requirement for completing graduate school, you must submit a thesis, which is a detailed research report. Your degree is in Education with a minor in Information Technology. Your thesis will center on generational learning styles, comparing the way students learn across the generations. Although you have not yet conducted your research, you suspect that students aged 55 and older have a very different way of learning than do younger students. You expect the use of technology in learning to be much more intimidating to older students who have not been exposed to such learning at a high level. As a researcher, however, you know that such suppositions must be supported or proven incorrect by research. As part of your thesis preparation, you are surveying a group of senior adults and a group of college students who are less than 25 years old. The local senior center will distribute your survey to seniors who are currently enrolled in a non-credit computer literacy course sponsored by the senior center. The same survey will be given to students enrolled in a computer literacy college course. The survey covers Windows 7 basics and includes the following steps. You should go over the steps before finalizing the survey instrument. This project follows the same set of skills as used in Hands-On Exercises 1, 2, and 3 in the chapter. Use Figure 48 as a reference as you complete this exercise.

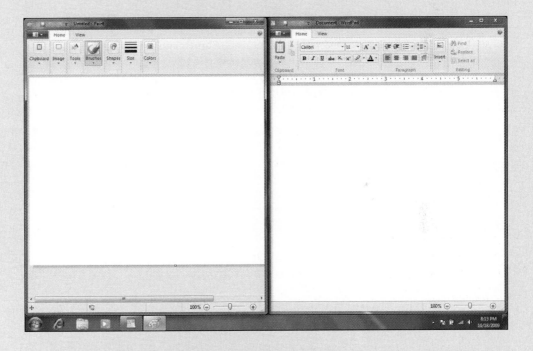

FIGURE 48 Paint and WordPad windows ➤

a. Click the **Start button**. Click **Control Panel**. Click **Change desktop background**. Make sure Picture location shows Windows Desktop Backgrounds. Scroll through the picture choices and select one. Click **Save Changes** if you are allowed to make a change to the desktop, or **Cancel** if you are not. Close all open windows.

b. Click the **Start button**. Point to **All Programs**. Click **Accessories**. Right-click **WordPad** and click **Pin to Taskbar**. Click outside the Start menu to remove it from view.

c. Click the **Start button**. Point to **All Programs**. Click **Accessories**. Right-click **Paint**. Click **Pin to Start Menu**. Click outside the Start menu to remove it from view.

d. Click the **Start button**. Point to **All Programs**. Click **Accessories**. Right-click and drag **Notepad** to the desktop. Release the mouse button. Click **Create shortcuts here**.

e. Click the **WordPad icon** on the taskbar. With WordPad still open, click the **Start button**. Click **Paint**. If you have recently opened Paint files, you may have to click Paint twice to open it.

f. Right-click an empty area of the taskbar. Click **Show windows side by side**. Compare your screen to Figure 48.

g. Click the **Close button** at the top right corner of the Paint window to close the program.

h. Click the **Maximize button** (middle control button) on the right side of the WordPad window to maximize the window.

i. Click the **Start button**. Click **Help and Support**. Click Browse Help. Click **Security and privacy**. Scroll down the list if necessary and click **Helping to protect your computer from viruses**. Click **How can I tell if my computer has a virus?**. Identify some symptoms of a virus.

j. Right-click an empty area of the taskbar. Click **Show windows stacked**. Click in the WordPad window and in your own words, list at least three virus symptoms.

k. Click the **Start button**. Point to **All Programs**. Click **Accessories**. Click **Snipping Tool**. Click the **arrow** beside *New*. Click **Full-screen Snip**. Click the **Save Snip button**. Scroll down the left side of the **Save As dialog box** and click to select the disk drive where you will save your student files. Click in the **File name box** and type **win01p1survey_LastnameFirstname**. Click **Save**.

l. Close all open windows without saving.

m. Right-click the **WordPad** icon on the taskbar. Click **Unpin this program from taskbar**. Click the **Start button**. Right-click **Paint**. Click **Unpin from Start Menu**. Click outside the Start menu to remove it from view.

n. Right-click the **Notepad icon** on the desktop. Click **Delete**. Confirm the deletion.

2 Silent Auction

As part of your responsibility as vice president of the National Youth Assembly of College Athletes, you are soliciting donated items for a silent auction at the national conference. You accept items and tag them with an estimated value and a beginning bid requirement. You will use a computer to keep a record of the donor, value, and minimum bid requirement. Because you will not always be in the office when an item is donated, you will configure the desktop and taskbar of the computer to simplify the job of data entry for anyone who happens to be at the desk. This project follows the same set of skills as used in Hands-On Exercises 1, 2, and 3 in the chapter. Use Figure 49 as a reference as you complete this exercise.

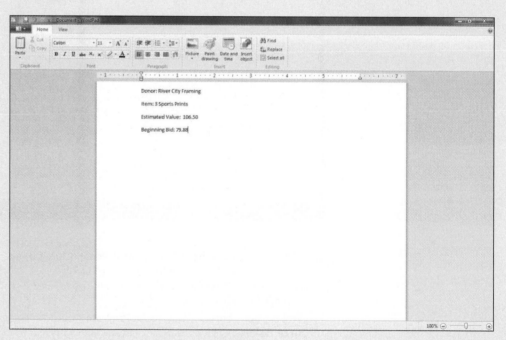

FIGURE 49 Silent Auction Items ➤

a. Click the **Start button**. Point to **All Programs**. Click **Accessories**. Right-click and drag WordPad to the desktop. Click **Create shortcuts here**.

b. Right-click an empty area of the taskbar. Click **Properties**. Click the **check box** beside *Auto-hide the taskbar* (if no check mark appears). Click **OK**.

c. Double-click the **WordPad icon** on the desktop. WordPad will open.
- Click the **Maximize button**. If no insertion point (blinking bar) appears in the upper-left corner of the white space, click to position it there.
- Type **Donor: River City Framing**. Press **Enter**.
- Type **Item: 3 Sports Prints**. Press **Enter**.
- Type **Estimated Value:**. Press **Spacebar**.

d. Click the **Start button**. Point to **All Programs**. Click **Accessories**. Click **Calculator**.

The estimated value of each print is $35.50, but the frames will be sold as a unit. Therefore, you need to determine the total value ($35.50 multiplied by 3). Because you are in the middle of typing a WordPad document, you do not want to close it. Instead, you will open the Calculator program and compute the value.

e. Using the mouse, click **35.50*3** and click =. The total value should show on the calculator. Minimize the Calculator.

f. In the WordPad document, type the total. Press **Enter**. Type **Beginning Bid:**. Press the spacebar.

g. Click the **Calculator icon** on the taskbar. The amount from step (e) should still be displayed on the Calculator. Click the **multiplication key** (*) and **.75**. Click =. Jot down the value shown on the Calculator and close the Calculator.

The beginning bid will be 75% of the estimated value. So the calculation should be Estimated Value multiplied by .75.

h. If necessary, click after the word *Bid:* in the WordPad window. Type the value that you recorded in step (g), rounded up to the nearest hundredth. Press **Enter**. Compare your screen to Figure 49.

i. Click the **Start button**. Click **Help and Support**. Maximize the Windows Help and Support window. Click in the **Search box** and type **WordPad**. Press **Enter**. Click **Using WordPad**. Click **Create, open, and save documents** on the right side. If necessary, click **Create, open, and save documents** to expand the detail. Look at the displayed table to determine how to save a document. Close Windows Help and Support.

j. As you were directed in the Help and Support tip, click the **WordPad button** (just to the left of the Home tab).
- Click **Save**.
- Scroll down the left side of the dialog box to Computer and click the disk drive where you save your student files. Proceed through any folder structure, as directed by your instructor.
- Click in the **File name box** and type **win01p2auction_LastnameFirstname**. You might first need to remove the current file name before typing the new one.
- Click **Save**.
- Close WordPad.

k. Right-click the taskbar. Click **Properties**. Click **Auto-hide the taskbar**. Click **OK**.

l. Right-click the **WordPad icon** on the desktop. Click **Delete**. Confirm the deletion.

MID-LEVEL EXERCISES

1 Junk Business

You and a college friend have signed on as a franchise for JUNKit, a company that purchases unwanted items and disposes of or recycles them. A recent pickup included a desktop computer that appeared to be reusable. Because you had a few spare parts and some hardware expertise, you rebuilt the computer and installed Windows 7. Now you will check the system to verify that it is workable and configured correctly.

a. Open WordPad and type as directed when you complete the following items.

b. Open the Action Center. Are there any alerts? Make note of them and close the Action Center. In the WordPad document, type **Step b:** and list any alerts or indicate that there are none. Press **Enter**.

c. Open Windows Defender and check to see when the last scan occurred. Click the WordPad icon on the taskbar, click in the document on the line following your response for Step b, type **Step c:**, and record when the last scan occurred. Press **Enter**. Right-click the **Windows Defender** icon on the taskbar and click **Close window**.

d. Check the firewall status. Is the firewall on? Close the System and Security window. If necessary, click in the WordPad document on the line following your response for Step c. Type **Step d:** and record whether the firewall is on or off. (Note that the firewall may not be on for the lab computer because the campus lab is likely to be behind another campus-wide firewall. Your computer at home is more likely to have the firewall turned on.) Press **Enter**.

e. Check Windows Update. When did the last update occur? Click the **WordPad** icon on the taskbar. If necessary, click in the WordPad document on the line following your response for Step d. Type **Step e:** and record the date of the last update. Press **Enter**. Right-click the Windows Update icon on the taskbar and click **Close window**.

f. Check for available desktop backgrounds. Identify one that you plan to use, but click **Cancel** without selecting it. Close any open windows other than WordPad. If necessary, click in the WordPad document on the line following your response for Step e. Type **Step f:** and list the name of the background that you would have selected in the WordPad document. Press **Enter**.

 **DISCOVER**

g. Open Help and Support. Find information on the Aero desktop. Specifically, identify a definition of the Aero desktop and requirements for its use (computer specifications and Windows 7 versions that support Aero). Going a little further, find out what Aero Shake is and how it could be beneficial in managing a desktop. Click the **WordPad** icon on the taskbar, type **Step g:**, and summarize your findings in the WordPad document. Press **Enter**.

h. Click the **Restore Down button** to reduce the size of the WordPad window. Snap the Windows Help and Support window to one side of the desktop and the WordPad document to the other.

i. Close the Windows Help and Support window. Save the WordPad document by clicking the **Save button** (second from left on the topmost row of the WordPad window). Scroll down in the left pane of the dialog box and click **Computer**. Double-click the disk drive where you save your student files (as directed by your instructor). Click in the **File name box** and type **win01m1junk_LastnameFirstname**. Click **Save**. Close WordPad.

2 Technical Writing

 **CREATIVE CASE**

You are employed as a software specialist with Wang Design, a firm that provides commercial and residential landscape design and greenscape services. The landscape designers use a wide array of software that assists with producing detailed plans and lawn layouts. The firm has just purchased several new computers, configured with Windows 7. Because the operating system is new to all employees, you have been assigned the task of producing a small easy-to-follow manual summarizing basic Windows 7 tasks. Use WordPad or Microsoft Word to produce a report, no more than 10 pages, based on the following topic outline. Where appropriate, use the Snipping Tool to include screen captures that illustrate a topic or process. Use this chapter and Windows Help and Support to find information for your report. Save your report as **win01m2writing_LastnameFirstname**.

1. Desktop Components
2. Customizing the Desktop
3. Windows Accessories
4. Windows Search

CAPSTONE EXERCISE

You are enrolled in a Directed Studies class as one of the final courses required for your degree. The class is projects-based, which means that the instructor assigns open-ended cases for students to manage and report on. You will prepare teaching materials for a Windows 7 community education class. The class is a new effort for the college, and given early enrollment figures, it appears that most students are over the age of 45 with very little computer background. Most students indicate that they have recently purchased a computer with Windows 7 and want to learn to work with the operating system at a minimal level. The class is short, only a couple of Saturday mornings, and it is fast approaching. In this exercise, you will prepare and test class material introducing students to the desktop, managing windows, working with accessory programs and security settings, getting help, and finding files. Your instructor wants screen shots of your progress, so you will use the Snipping Tool to prepare those.

Explore the Desktop and Manage Windows

The instructor will spend the first hour of class introducing students to the Windows 7 desktop and to the concept of windows. He will assume that students are complete novices, so he wants an outline that begins with the basics. You have prepared the series of steps given below. You will go through those steps, preparing a screen shot to accompany your submission.

a. Auto arrange icons on the desktop (if they are not already set to auto arrange).

b. Create a desktop shortcut for the Notepad program.

c. Pin the WordPad program to the taskbar.

d. Open the Notepad shortcut. If necessary, restore down the window so that it is not maximized.

e. Open WordPad from the taskbar. If necessary, restore down the window so that it is not maximized.

f. Snap each window to opposing sides of the desktop.

g. Show the windows stacked.

h. Use the Snipping Tool to capture a copy of the screen. Save it as **win01c1desktop_LastnameFirstname**.

i. Close all open windows.

Work with Accessory Programs and Security Settings

The instructor wants to make sure students understand that some software is included with a Windows 7 installation. Because using any type of software most often involves Internet access, you know that the class must include instruction on security risks and solutions. You have prepared some notes and will test them in the steps that follow.

a. Open WordPad. Maximize the window, if necessary. Students in class will be instructed to type a paragraph on Windows 7 security features. Use Windows 7 Help and Support if necessary to identify Windows 7 security features, and then compose a paragraph in the WordPad document. Minimize WordPad but do not close it.

b. Open Paint. Maximize the window, if necessary. Click the top half of the **Brushes button**. Click and drag to write **your name** in the *Paint* area. Click the top half of the **Select button**. Click and drag in a rectangle around your name. Click **Copy**. Close Paint without saving.

c. Click the **WordPad icon** on the taskbar. Click the top half of the **Paste button** to add your "signature" to the paragraph.

d. Save the WordPad document as **win01c1paragraph_ LastnameFirstname**.

e. Close WordPad.

Get Help and Find Files

You know from personal experience that things usually work well when an instructor is available to help. You also know that as students leave the Windows 7 class, they will have questions and must know how to find help themselves. They will also undoubtedly misplace files. The steps that follow should help them understand how to get help and how to find files, programs, and folders.

a. Browse Help and Support to find information on the Start menu.

b. Search Help and Support to find a description of remote assistance.

c. Minimize the Windows Help and Support window.

d. Click the **Start button**, click in the **Start menu Search box**, and type **Word**. You will search for any program with the word *word* in the program name. At the very least, you should see *WordPad* in the results list. Click the program name to open it. If WordPad is maximized, restore it down to less than full size.

e. Click the **Help and Support icon** on the taskbar to open the window.

f. Show the windows stacked.

g. Use the Snipping Tool to capture the screen, saving it as **win01c1help_LastnameFirstname**. Close all open windows.

h. Unpin the WordPad icon from the taskbar.

i. Delete the NotePad icon from the desktop.

Speech Class

GENERAL CASE

You are taking a Speech class and must develop a demonstration speech, complete with a sheet of notes. A demonstration speech is one in which you teach or direct the class on how to do something. Because Windows 7 is a relatively new operating system, you decide to demonstrate some of its features. You will use WordPad to record a few notes that will help you make your presentation. After completing your notes, save the document as **win01b1speech_LastnameFirstname** in a location as directed by your instructor. In a 1, 2, 3 fashion (listing your points in numerical order), provide directions to the class on how to:

- Customize the desktop with a background and screen saver
- Pin programs to the taskbar and the Start menu
- Use the Start menu Search box to find and open a program that you think is installed on your computer system
- Get Help on an item related to Windows 7
- Make sure your computer is protected against spyware and hacking

Campus Chatter

RESEARCH CASE

As a reporter for the college newspaper *Campus Chatter,* you are responsible for the education section. Each month, you contribute a short article on an educational topic. This month, you will summarize a feature of Windows 7. You are having writer's block, however, and need a nudge, so you will use the Internet for an idea. Click Start, All Programs, Accessories, Getting Started. Click Go online to learn more. You will be directed to the Windows 7 Web site. Peruse some links, locate a topic of interest, and use WordPad to write a minimum one-page typed report on a topic related to Windows 7. Save the report as **win01b2chatter_ LastnameFirstname** in a location as directed by your instructor.

Laptop Logic

DISASTER RECOVERY

Your job in sales with an educational software company requires a great deal of travel. You depend on a laptop computer for most of what you do, from keeping sales records to connecting with an overhead projector when you make presentations to groups. In short, you would be lost without your computer. A recent scare, when you temporarily misplaced the laptop, has led you to consider precautions you can take to make sure your computer and its data are protected. Since you have a little free time before leaving for your next trip, you will use Windows 7 Help and Support to explore some suggestions on protecting your laptop. Open Help and Support and search for information on *protecting a laptop*. Create a one- to two-page typed report covering two topics. First, describe how you would protect data (including passwords and financial information) on your laptop. Second, provide some suggestions on steps you can take to make sure you do not lose your laptop or have it stolen. Use WordPad to record the report, saving the report as **win01b3laptop_LastnameFirstname** in a location as directed by your instructor.

GLOSSARY

Action Center A Windows 7 component that monitors maintenance and security settings, alerting a user when necessary. It provides alerts in pop-ups from an icon in the notification area.

Aero Flip 3D A feature that shows open windows in a rotating 3D stack from which you can click to bring a window to view on the desktop.

Aero Peek A preview of an open window, shown when you place the mouse pointer over the taskbar icon without clicking. Aero Peek also enables you to minimize all open windows, showing the desktop temporarily.

Calculator A Windows 7 accessory program that acts as a handheld calculator with four different views—standard, scientific, programming, and statistical.

Desktop The screen display that appears after you turn on a computer. It contains icons and a taskbar.

Dialog box A window that opens when you are accomplishing a task that requires your confirmation or interaction.

File property A file identifier, such as author or date created.

Firewall Software or hardware that protects a computer from unauthorized access.

Gadget A desktop item that can represent things that change, such as the weather or a clock. Gadgets also include such things as puzzles and games.

Help and Support A built-in library of help topics that is available from the Start menu. Using Help and Support, you can get assistance with specific questions or broad topics.

Icon A small picture on the desktop that represents a program, file, or folder.

Jump List A list of actions or resources associated with an open window button or a pinned icon on the taskbar.

Notepad A text-editing program built in to Windows 7.

Notification area An area located on the right side of the taskbar. It displays icons for background programs and system resources. It also provides status information in pop-up windows.

Operating system Software that directs computer activities, performing such tasks as recognizing keyboard input, sending output to a display, and keeping track of files and folders.

Paint A graphics program, built in to Windows 7 that enables you to create drawings and open picture files.

Pin The process of placing icons of frequently used programs on the taskbar or on the Start menu.

Screen saver A series of images or a graphic display that continually moves over the screen when the computer has been idle for a specified period of time. Screen savers can be used for security purposes to keep others from viewing computer contents.

Shortcut A link, or pointer, to a program or computer resource.

Snap A feature that arranges windows automatically on the left and right sides of the desktop.

Snip A screen display that has been captured and displayed by screen capture software.

Snipping Tool A Windows 7 accessory program that captures screen displays for saving or sharing.

Spyware Software that is installed from the Internet, usually without the user's permission. It can gather information for marketing purposes, and is sometimes capable of changing computer settings and recording keystrokes.

Start button A button located at the left side of the taskbar. Click the Start button to display the Start menu.

Start menu A menu that is displayed when you click the Start button. It is a list of programs, folders, utilities, and tasks.

Tag A file property, such as a rating, that a user can apply to a file for identification purposes.

Taskbar The horizontal bar located at the bottom of the desktop. It displays icons for open windows, a Start button, pinned icons, and a notification area.

Title bar A horizontal bar that appears at the top of each open window. The title bar identifies the window contents.

Toolbar A collection of icons or items, usually displayed in a horizontal fashion, from which you can make selections.

User Account Control (UAC) A Windows feature that asks a user's permission before allowing any changes to computer settings.

Window A rectangular, bordered area of space on the desktop that represents a program, system resource, or data.

Windows Defender An antispyware program that is installed along with Windows 7.

Windows Updates Software patches, or fixes, provided by Microsoft, that prevent or correct problems. Many updates focus on security concerns.

WordPad A basic word processing program built in to Windows 7.

Index

A

Accessories (accessory programs), 23–26, 43
Action Center, 10, 26–27, 43
    alerts, 10, 26–27, 43
    defined, 10
Address toolbar, 7–8
Aero Flip 3D, 13–14
Aero Peek, 5–6
Alerts, Action Center and, 10, 26–27, 43
Antispyware software, 23, 26–27, 43
Antivirus software, 9, 26–27, 29, 43
Application software, 1–2
Arranging icons, 4
Auto arranging icons, 4
Auto–hiding taskbar, 7

B

Background (desktop background)
    changing, 10
    slide shows for, 12
Built–in categories (for desktop customization), 10
Built–in programs (on Windows 7), 23–26
Buttons
    close button, 12–13
    command buttons, 15
    Help button, 39
    maximize button, 12–13
    minimize button, 12–13
    New Note button, 25
    option buttons, 15
    show desktop button, 14
    Start button, 5–6

C

Calculator (accessory program), 1, 3, 24–25, 43
Calendar (gadget), 4
Case study, 1
Cedar Cove Elementary School, 1
Check boxes, 15
Children, parental controls feature and, 30
Clipboard, 26
Clock (gadget), 4

Close button (X), 12–13
Colors
    for windows, 10
    Paint program and, 1, 24
Command buttons, 15
Components
    of desktop, 2–4
    of dialog boxes, 15
    of windows, 12–13
Computers
    as microcomputer systems, 2
    purposes for, 23
Creating
    background slide shows, 12
    folders, 3
Customization
    computers and, 23
    desktop, 10–12
    taskbar icons, 5–6
    UAC, 27–28

D

Defender (Windows Defender), 26–28, 43
Degrees
    Computer Information Systems, 1
    Information Technology, 45
Deleting
    gadgets, 4
    icons, 3
    Sticky Notes, 25
Desktop, 2–12
    components, 2–4
    customization of, 10–12
    defined, 2, 43
Desktop background
    changing, 10
    slide shows for, 12
Dialog boxes, 14–15
    components of, 15
    defined, 14
    Help button and, 39
    Print, 15
    Screen Saver, 10–11
Drawing feature (Paint program), 1, 24

E

Easy Connect, 39
Elementary school case study, 1
Expanding searches, 36–37
Expanding windows, 13

F

File properties, 35
Firewalls, 26, 29–30, 43
Folder creation, 3
Fundamentals (Windows 7), 2–12

G

Gadgets Gallery, 4
Games, 4

H

Hackers, 23, 26, 43
Hands–on exercises, 16–22, 31–34, 40–42
Help and Support, 35, 37–39, 43
Help button, 39

I

Icons
    Aero Peek and, 5–6
    auto arranging, 4
    defined, 2
    deleting, 3
    pinning, 8–9
    renaming, 3
    taskbar, 5–6
Indexing options, 36
Information Technology degree, 45

J

Jump List, 8–9

K

Key terms, 43

L

Left pane (Start menu), 6–7
Links toolbar, 7
List boxes, 15
List, of toolbars, 7–8

M

Maintenance, Action Center and, 10, 26–27, 43
Maximize button, 12–13
Maximizing windows, 12–13
Microcomputer systems, 2
Microsoft Windows web site, 4
Microsoft Word, 23, 48
Minimize button, 12–13
Monitoring, Action Center and, 10, 26–27, 43
Moving gadgets, 4

N

Naming icons, 3
Narrowing searches, 36–37
New Note button, 25
Notepad (accessory program), 23
Notes, Sticky, 25
Notification area, 5, 9–10
Number of copies option, 15
Numeric keypad, 24

O

Online
gadgets, 4
Help and Support, 39
Microsoft Windows web site, 4
Opacity level, of gadgets, 4
Operating systems, 2
defined, 2
Windows 7, 2, 23
Windows Updates and, 29
Option buttons, 15

P

Paint (accessory program), 1, 24
Parental controls, 30
Pencil tool (Paint program), 24
Personalize, 10
Picture Puzzle (gadget), 4
Pictures
background slide show with, 12
Paint program and, 1, 24
picture location, 10–11
Pinned programs, 8–9
Pop–up window, status information and, 9
Previewing windows (Aero Peek), 5–6
Print dialog box, 15
Programmer view (Calculator program), 24–25
Programs (software programs/ application software), 23–26
accessories, 23–26, 43
application software and, 1–2
Calculator, 1, 3, 24–25, 43
defined, 23
firewalls, 26, 29–30, 43

Notepad, 23
operating system and, 2, 23
Paint, 1, 24
pinned, 8–9
Snipping Tool, 25–26, 43
spyware protection, 23, 26–27, 43
Sticky Notes, 25
virus protection, 9, 26–27, 29, 43
Windows Updates and, 29
WordPad, 23
Puzzles, 4

R

Remote Assistance, 37, 39
Renaming icons, 3
Resizing
gadgets, 4
windows, 12–13
Ribbon (Paint program), 24
Right pane (Start menu), 6–7

S

Saved searches, 37
Scientific view (Calculator program), 24–25
Screen savers, 10–11
Search box, 6, 35–37, 43
Searches, 35–37, 43
expanding, 36–37
Help and Support and, 38
narrowing, 36–37
saving, 37
Security, 26–30, 43
Action Center and, 10, 26–27, 43
firewalls and, 26, 29–30, 43
hackers and, 23, 26, 43
parental controls feature and, 30
settings for, 26–30
UAC and, 27–28
Windows Defender and, 23, 26–28
Windows Updates and, 29
Selecting
picture location, 10–11
screen savers, 10–11
Shortcuts
adding, 3
defined, 3
Jump List and, 8–9
Show desktop button, 14
Sizing
gadgets, 4
windows, 12–13
Slide shows, for desktop background, 12
Snap (feature), 14
Snipping Tool (accessory program), 25–26, 43

Snips, 25
Software operating systems, 2, 23
Spin arrows, 15
Spyware, 23, 26–27, 43
Standard view (Calculator program), 24–25
Start button, 5–6
Start menu, 6–7
left pane, 6–7
pinning programs to, 9
right pane, 6–7
Status information, Notification area and, 9
Sticky Notes (accessory program), 25

T

Tags, 35, 43
Taskbar, 4–10
defined, 5
exploring, 4–10
hiding, 7
pinning programs to, 8–9
Taskbar icons, customization of, 5–6
Terms, key, 43
Text boxes, 15
3D window stack (Aero Flip 3D), 13–14
Tips
background slide show, creation of, 12
icons, auto arranging, 4
parental controls, 30
pinning items (to Start Menu), 9
Sticky Notes, 25
task bar icons, customizing, 6
taskbar, hiding, 7
windows, expanding, 13
windows, maximizing, 12–13
Title bar, 12–13
Toolbars, 7–8

U

UAC (User Account Control), 27–28
Unpinning items, 8–9
Updates, Windows, 29
User Account Control (UAC), 27–28

V

Vertical expansion, of windows, 13
Viruses, 9, 26–27, 29, 43

W

Window color (feature), 10
Window(s), 12–15
Aero Flip 3D and, 13–14
colors for, 10
components, 12–13
defined, 2
dialog boxes as, 14

expanding, 13
managing, 12–15, 43
maximizing, 12–13
minimizing, 12–13
previewing, 5–6
resizing, 12–13
Snap feature and, 14
Snipping Tool and, 25–26, 43

Windows 7 (Microsoft)
    Accessories, 23–26
    as operating system, 2, 23
    fundamentals, 2–12
    security, 27–30
Windows accessories, 23–26, 43
Windows Defender, 26–28, 43
Windows firewall, 26, 29–30, 43

Windows Remote Assistance, 39
Word (Microsoft Word), 23, 48
WordPad (accessory program), 1, 23

X

X (close button), 12–13